D0787402

Historical Dictionary of
Panama

by
Basil C. and Anne K. Hedrick

Latin American Historical Dictionaries, No. 2

The Scarecrow Press, Inc.
Metuchen, N. J.   1970

Latin American Historical Dictionaries Series
Edited by A. Curtis Wilgus

1. Moore, Richard E. Historical Dictionary of Guatemala.
1967.

2. Hedrick, Basil C. and Anne K. Historical Dictionary of
Panama. 1970.

Editor's Foreword

The assignment given to the compilers of the
Historical Dictionaries was to select arbitrarily material for
inclusion which was logical and justifiable, as well as com-
prehensive, so that each resulting volume would constitute
a helpful, balanced, but not exhaustive guide and ready
reference to pertinent topics concerning a particular Latin
American country. However, the series does not constitute
an encyclopedia, and much information may be supplemented
from factual sources. In this volume the authors have
indicated in their bibliography references for further
searching.

Unlike other Latin American countries, Panama has
had a short national period of independence. This fact has
both simplified and complicated the selection of material
here included. In the colonial era under Spain, and in the
subsequent period when it was a turbulent province of
Columbia, Panamanians, as we think of them today, did not
exist. During Panama's independent life, less than three
generations, there has unfortunately been little time for
mature political, economic and cultural advancement. More-
over, the Canal Zone, bisecting the country, has been a
fracturing factor affecting all phases of national life and
development and has led to an unusual awareness of United
States influence, potential and actual, which has intruded
into all aspects of Panama's recent history.

These facts have been kept in mind by Dr. and Mrs.
Hedrick in preparing their volume. Both authors have been
interested for several years in Latin America in general,
and in Mexico and Central America particularly, and they
have jointly carried on research in these areas. Professor
Hedrick has a special interest in history, archaeology and
anthropology, and at present he is Director of the Museum
at the Southern Illinois University at Carbondale.
Previously he served as Assistant Director of the Latin
American Institute at that institution and before that as
Assistant Director of the School of Inter-American Studies

at the University of Florida, where he received the M.A. degree in history. His Ph.D. is from the Inter-American University in Mexico. He is the author of several publications in his fields of interest, and he holds the honorary TCEA from Panama. Anne, his wife, has been his collaborator in research and writing as well as in his travels in Latin America, Europe and Southeast Asia. Mrs. Hedrick is also a trained teacher and she has occupied a number of important positions in and out of academic circles. They have effectively combined their talents in preparing this Dictionary, and it has been a great personal pleasure for the Editor to have been associated with them.

A. Curtis Wilgus
Emeritus Director
School of Inter-American Studies
University of Florida

Introduction

The Historical Dictionary of Panama is a compilation
of historical facts and figures, blended with a potpourri of
salient facts from various disciplines which, when taken together, are aimed to provide a source book of information
on Panama which should be of benefit to any social scientist.
The primary objective of the volume is to provide factual
information on persons, places, events, geographical and
political subdivisions, and some contemporary events and
statistics--all pertinent to the Republic of Panama. The research for the publication is based on many years of experi-
ence throughout Latin America and particularly upon detailed
study during 1969. The latest information possible was
gathered on a fact-finding trip to Panama by the authors in
June of that year.

No book of this nature can be exhaustive, for the
facts pertaining to any one facet of the history of any given
nation could fill many volumes. Instead, we have endeavored
to cull out materials which we would like to have included,
but which, for the sake of relative brevity and corresponding
applicability, were judged not worthy of inclusion here.

The arrangement of the entries is alphabetical, with
appropriate cross-references for abbreviations, pseudonyms,
variant spellings, and acronyms. The list of presidents
includes every president who has served the Republic, whether
in a regular, temporary, transient, or acting status. Aside
from present and past presidents who are still living, the
only other contemporary individuals listed are those of outstanding literary, artistic, or diplomatic note.

With the exception of early Spanish colonizers and a
few important leaders pertinent to the development of the
Republic, the only persons listed are Panamanians.

Geographical entries include all provinces, districts,
cabeceras, major or important towns and cities, rivers,
lakes, and mountain peaks and volcanoes.

Spanish words which have been included are limited to Panamanianisms and, in a few cases, historic terminology necessary to the understanding of the history of Panama.

All current statistics, unless otherwise noted, are taken from official Panamanian Government sources, generally from the Contraloría General de la República. If statistical errors occur, they should at least be uniform in nature.

We wish to thank Dr. Alfredo Castillero Calvo, Director of the Comisión de Estudios Interdisciplinarios para el Desarrollo de la Nacionalidad and Chairman of the Department of History of the National University of Panama, for his invaluable help in obtaining many of the elusive facts and figures contained in this book. Our thanks also to the nameless but delightful young lady at the Instituto Panameño de Turismo who tried so hard to satisfy two persistent gringos in their quest for information. To Mrs. Judy Grimes and Dr. Larry Grimes, both of whom worked far beyond the call, our sincere appreciation for their aid in preparation and critical reading of the manuscript. And, to Anne L. Hedrick, our appreciation for her forebearance with two parents buried up to their necks in cards and papers.

B. C. H.
A. K. H.

ACABANGARSE. To feel afflicted, oppressed or vexed.

ACCION COMUNAL. A political group backed by Independents
and Conservatives and led by Harmodio Arias on a
platform opposed to graft and tyranny. Early in 1931,
the group overthrew Florencio Harmodio Arosemena's
government, and aided in the installation of Dr. Ricardo
J. Alfaro as chief executive until elections in 1932 put
Harmodio Arias in office.

ACLA. Located on the Caribbean Coast, in the Territory of
San Blas, Acla is the town where, in 1519, Pedrarias
had Balboa beheaded.

ACONCHABARSE. To make a secret, generally illicit pact
between two or more people.

ACOQUINADO. Frightened, submissive, dominated.

ACHOLADO. A word applied to the hair of the cholo or
indigenous farmer, or to any person having hair with
such characteristics.

ADELANTADO. Most important official in newly acquired
territory, who usually held the title of governor until
the arrival of the viceroy. The levels of power
were: adelantado mayor, governor with judicial,
administrative and military power; adelantado menor
or fronterizo, often appointed by a governor to act as
military head at outposts in distant regions;
adelantado de la corte or del rey, official representative of the king; adelantado del mar, entrusted to
those in command of an expedition, granting them the
title of governor of the territories they discovered or
conquered.

AGUADULCE. One of six distritos in the Province of Coclé.
Its cabecera is Aguadulce.

AGUADULCE.   Cabecera of the Aguadulce District.   Population: 4, 397.   Lying approximately 21 miles southwest
of Penonomé, Aguadulce is a colonial town with hand-
some private residences and public buildings and has
become a collection and way station for truckers.   It
has lodging facilities and a restricted airport which
aid in the growth of the town as an important commercial center in the area.

AGUAITAR.   To scrutinize, to pry, to examine closely.

AGUAMASA.   Applied to a mean, stupid individual.

AGUEVADO.   A very wide-spread vulgarism meaning stupid,
ignorant, devoid of all ambition.

ALANJE.   One of twelve distritos in the Province of
Chiriquí.   Its cabecera is Alanje.

ALANJE.   Cabecera of the Alanje District.   Population: 544.

ALCALDE.   The mayor and judge during the colonial
period.   Alcaldes mayores were royal appointees
chosen at the recommendation of the viceroy for a
period of three years.   Alcaldes ordinarios were
elected officials in each town, to handle routine
duties.   The alcalde de la hermandad was a police
magistrate for rural areas.   The ward or parish
supervisor for larger towns was the alcalde de barrio.
During the national period, the alcalde was the
municipio political leader appointed by the national
government through the departmental governors.   Since
1944 the position has been elective.

ALEMAN, Roberto R.   Panamanian Ambassador to the
United States, 1968-

ALFARO, Eloy.   Born in 1866, Eloy Alfaro, an Ecuadorian
of great ability, became chief executive of Ecuador
in 1895 following a revolution against the Cordero
government.   He ruled as "Supreme Chief" for two
years, then changed his title to President and ruled
until 1901.   He resumed office in 1906 following
another revolution and ruled until 1911 when he resigned and left for Europe.   Anarchy followed and he
was persuaded to return to take office, but as he
strove to regain control of the government, he was
murdered on January 28, 1912.   He is mentioned in a

history of Panama owing to the fact that he is widely
revered in the nation as a great political martyr. He
had close ties with that nation, having spent much
time in the country, especially during periods of
exile, when he used Panama as his base of operations.
He is often referred to as a "Citizen of the Americas"
and as the prototype Apostle of Pan-Americanism.
The Headquarters of the Eloy Alfaro International
Foundation are located in Panama City.

ALFARO, Dr. Ricardo, b. 1882. A most capable diplomat,
philologist, historian, and expert on international
law, Dr. Alfaro headed the government in 1931-32,
following the overthrow of Florencio Harmodio
Arosemena. He held office until elections on October
1, 1932. He was a member of the International
Court of Justice at The Hague. In 1936, he negotiated
a treaty with Washington providing for the payment
by the U.S. of the Canal rent in balboas (Panamanian
currency) instead of in dollars, at the rate equivalent
to the gold dollar of that date. The U.S. also agreed
to give up the right of intervention in Panama but
would guarantee that country's independence. This
treaty was ratified by the U.S. and subsequently revised in 1955. In the elections of 1940, Alfaro headed
a coalition of liberals and socialists in hope of break-
ing the control of the conservatives. However, following a spate of disorders and violence prior to and
during the election (allegedly incited by the backers
of Arnulfo Arias), Alfaro was defeated by Arias, who
took office on October 1, 1940.

ALGUACIL MAYOR. The local constable in colonial Spanish
America, a lucrative post often obtained by purchase.

ALMAGRO, Diego de. Sailed on Pedrarias' expedition from
Spain to the Isthmus in 1514. Entered into partner-
ship with Pizarro in a farming venture. Pizarro and
Almagro were linked by their illiteracy, unknown
parentage, and adventuresome natures. Almagro led
an expedition to conquer Chile in 1535, but was forced
to return to Peru following terrible hardships. He
reached as far south as the present-day Santiago.
Civil war developed between the Pizarros (brothers)
and the Almagros (father and son), which led to the
execution of Almagro, Sr., in 1538 and Almagro, Jr.,
in 1542.

AMACHINARSE. To be sad, cowardly, or lacking in spirit.

AMADOR GUERRERO, Manuel. Chosen by a national convention as first constitutional President of Panama
(1904-1908). His administration was initially supported by a coalition of Liberals and Conservatives,
but the Liberals soon threatened a coup d'etat. This
was avoided only by intervention of the American
Minister. Amador Guerrero requested the U.S.
Government to supervise the elections in Panama
in 1905. The U.S. declined, but three years later
U.S. troops were landed to oversee the voting during
that year. Perhaps the largest problem of Amador's
regime was that of sanitation. It was under his rule
that Gorgas, et al., spearheaded the drive to ob-
literate malaria and yellow fever.

AMERICAN PRESIDENTS' MEETING OF PANAMA. July 21-
22, 1956. see DECLARATION OF PANAMA (1956).

ANDREVE, Guillermo, 1879-1940. A leading Modernist
writer, Andreve was a short story writer and essay-
ist. His literary review El heraldo del istmo,
founded in 1904, brought him his greatest fame.

ANGU. Banana puree.

ANGUIZOLA, Santiago, 1899- . A writer of the Nativist
school, Anguizola wrote poetry which expressed a
reaction against modern cultural influences. He was
negatively affected by the incursion of Yankees and
the Canal.

AÑINGOTARSE. To squat, or to sit cowering.

ANTON. One of six distritos in the Province of Coclé.
Its cabecera is Antón.

ANTON. Cabecera of the Antón District. Population: 1,876.

APACHURRAR. To flatten, or crush.

APERCOLLAR. To embrace.

ARACHA. Cockroach.

ARAUJO, José Agustín. A leading political figure and

member of the 1903 provisional junta of government
which was formed on the declaration of independence
of Panama from Colombia.

ARCHAEOLOGY. Archaeology and ethnology in Panama are
still in a state of embryonic development. Though
famous American and Panamanian archaeologists
have worked in Panama, there is little of a definitive
picture yet drawn. When the Spaniards landed in
what is today Panama, the area was inhabited by
many Indian "tribes," the most important belonging
to the Cuna, Guaymí, and Chocó groups. These
groups had developed their cultural and social organi-
zations to a relatively high point. Archaeologists
are in general agreement that the Isthmus was used
as a grandiose highway between Central and South
America and perhaps as a link to North America.
It seems apparent, however, that no permanent
settlement took place on the Isthmus until a few
hundred years before the birth of Christ, when agri-
culturists started a few sparse, semi-permanent
villages. The most outstanding artifactual remains
(gold, ceramic, and stone sculpture), have been
found in the Provinces of Chiriquí, Veraguas, and
Coclé. The National Museum of Panama, founded
in 1925, is the preserver of the pre-Colombian
cultural remains in Panama.

ARIAS, Arnulfo, b. 1902. Thrice President of the Republic,
Arias (brother of Harmodio Arias) has had a stormy
political career. Arias defeated Ricardo J. Alfaro
for the presidency in 1940, and soon demonstrated
his extreme nationalism and propensity to friendship
for Hitler. He was deposed by the Guardia Nacional
in a bloodless coup during October, 1941. He attempted to maintain formal neutrality during World
War II by refusing to allow the arming of American-
owned ships under Panamanian registry. This led
to his first overthrow. Dr. Arias returned to the
Presidency in 1948 following the death of President
Arosemena and a circus-like succession of transitory
presidents. He was installed by the police and ratified by the National Election Jury as retroactive
winner of the 1948 elections. On May 9-10, he was
overthrown by revolution which broke out following
his announcement of the impending suspension of the
1946 constitution. He was later formally impeached.

He was again declared winner of the stormy elections of 1968, receiving 55% of the votes as announced
by the National Elections Tribunal. Arias was inaugurated on October 1, 1968, but was deposed once
again by the Guardia Nacional on October 12, 1968.
This was his shortest term of office.

ARIAS, Harmodio, 1886-1962. One of the leaders of the
Revolution of 1931, which overthrew the regime of
Florencio Harmodio Arosemena, Harmodio Arias
was elected President in 1932, succeeding the provisional government of Dr. Ricardo Alfaro. The
most important event of Arias' administration was a
new treaty with the U.S. (1936). This treaty,
negotiated by Ricardo Alfaro, and ratified in 1939,
was a distinct step forward in Panama's national
pride and material interests. Arias left office peace-
fully in 1936.

ARIAS, Tomás. A leading political figure and member of
the 1903 provisional junta of government which was
formed upon the declaration of independence of
Panama from Colombia.

ARIAS DAVILA, Pedro see PEDRARIAS.

ARIAS de AVILA, Pedro see PEDRARIAS.

ARJONA, J.E. Born in Pesé, Panama in 1887, Dr. Arjona
was educated at New York University and Harlem
Hospital in the United States. He was head of the
department of urinology at the Hospital Santo Tomás
from 1914 to 1939. He also headed the department
of venereal prophylaxis in Panama City from 1919-
1929. He was the owner of two private clinics,
President of the first convention Partido Nacional
Revolucionario, and president of the first Panamanian postal congress. He became director
general of post and telegraph in 1936.

AROSEMENA, Florencio Harmodio. President, 1928-1931,
succeeding Rodolfo Chiari. Owing to a breakdown
in party lines, government had become a personality
cult. Elections and true opposition were virtually
impossible. These circumstances, abetted by world
depression, led to the Revolution of 1931. On
January 2 of that year, a group of the President's

opponents seized control of the Capital and, following
brief but violent fighting, a semblance of constitutional
government returned under the provisional regime of
Dr. Ricardo Alfaro.

AROSEMENA, Juan Demóstenes. In the election of June,
1936, Juan Demóstenes Arosemena was elected chief
executive following one of the most closely contested
elections in the history of Panama. Initially declared
ineligible on a technicality by the National Elections
Jury, Arosemena, with backing from the incumbent
Harmodio Arias, was ultimately declared the winner
over the vociferous protests of his opponent, Domingo
Díaz. Arosemena, who is said to have had pro-
Fascist leanings, died in December, 1939 and was
succeeded by Dr. Augusto S. Boyd, the Vice-President.

AROSEMENA, Justo, 1817-1896. An influential writer of
political literature in Panama, Arosemena was a
statesman, scholar, and a proponent of nationalism.

AROSEMENA, Mariano, 1794-1868. One of the outstanding
historians of Panama.

AROSEMENA, Pablo. Served as President from September,
1910, until October, 1912, named by the National
Assembly to fill out the term of the deceased José
Domingo de Obaldía. Arosemena actually succeeded
Carlos Antonio Mendoza who became temporary
executive following de Obaldía's demise.

ARRAIJAN. One of ten distritos in the Province of Panama.
Its cabecera is Arraiján.

ARRAIJAN. Cabecera of the Arraiján District. Population:
1, 866.

ARRECOCHINAR. To corner a person or animal, impeding
escape.

ARRIERA. A large, reddish ant. Lives in underground
galleries, coming out in large bands to hunt food,
generally leaves. Often ruins gardens and flower
beds.

ARROCERO. A rice-eating bird which, if lacking rice,

feeds on other grains.   Considered a pest by the farmers.

ARROCHA GRAELL, Catalino. Born in Aguadulce, Panama in 1893, Arrocha attended the Instituto Nacional and the University of Chile, receiving an advanced teaching credential in 1920. He was under-secretary of education from 1923 to 1924, and also in 1932. He was under-secretary of education and agriculture from 1936 to 1940. He was also inspector general of education from 1933 to 1936 and president of the Instituto Nacional from 1940- . He wrote the Historia de la independencia de Panamá, 1821-1903.

ASPINALL. A town founded in 1850 which became Colón in 1890. Named in honor of one of its founders. See   COLON.

ATALAYA. One of eleven distritos in the Province of Veraguas. Its cabecera is Atalaya.

ATALAYA. Cabecera of the Atalaya District. Population: 902.

AUDIENCIA. The audiencia, a counterpoise to authority of the viceroys and captains general, was a judicial, executive, and consultative body. In the first capacity, it was the highest court of appeal and was presided over by the viceroy or captain general. During the vacancy of the local ruler, it assumed an executive role. At all times it had the right of direct communication with Spain over the head of local authorities. Finally, it frequently met with the governor as a consultative body as a kind of cabinet or council of state. The members of the audiencia enjoyed great prestige, generally received large compensations, and held themselves aloof from all local interest. Audiencias which were located at seats of government not presided over by a viceroy or captain general were given the name presidencia and the presiding official was given the title of presidente, e.g., the presidencia of Quito. An important duty of all audiencias was the protection of the rights of Indians. Panama's first audiencia was established in 1535 but seven years later came under the viceroyalty of Peru. Later, the Audiencia de los Confines was moved

from Panama to Honduras, then to Guatemala in
1549, returning to Panama during the years 1564-
1566. Next to the viceroys, the audiencia was
probably the most potent political and governing
institution in the government of the New World for
the initial 100 years after Spanish incursion.

AVIVATO. Applied to a person who lives off of others. A
"leech."

AYALA, Manuel José de, 1728-1805. Eminent jurist and
outstanding writer of the eighteenth century, Ayala
dealt mainly with social problems of the day.

AZTECS. A people of Central Mexico who, having
established a great centralized confederation under
an "emperor," were carrying on trade on a local
basis with tribes as far south as Panama when the
Spaniards arrived in the New World.

AZULEJO. A bird of blue and grey plumage, of which
there are various species, e. g., cyanospiza cyanea.

-B-

BACHICHE. A slightly contemptuous name given to Italian
immigrants in Panama.

BAJAREQUE. A fine mist or moisture always in the air
where the winds from the Atlantic and Pacific meet.
Also, walls made of cane, palm, or other vegetable
material, used in rural dwellings.

BAJO BOQUETE. Cabecera of the Boquete District. Population: 1,948.

BALBOA, Vasco Núñez de, 1474-1519. Spanish explorer
and adventurer who is credited with being the first
Caucasian to discover the South Sea (Pacific) at the
Gulf of San Miguel. On the discovery, he took
possession of the South Sea and all the lands bordering it in the name of the King of Spain. Named
Governor of Darién and instrumental in Spanish
settlement of the area, Balboa married Pedrarias'
daughter (who was in Spain) by proxy in order to
keep peace between them. Nevertheless, Balboa

was executed by the order of Pedrarias in 1519.

BALBOA. Monetary unit of Panama. On a par with the U. S. dollar. Divided into 100 centésimos.

BALBOA. One of ten distritos in the Province of Panama. Its cabecera is San Miguel.

BALBOA. Also, Balboa Heights. This city of 14,000 (1960 census) is the administrative capital of the Canal Zone, and is the largest U. S. -controlled city within the Zone. It is the western terminus of the Canal.

BALBOA MONUMENT. Balboa Monument, dedicated September 29, 1924, overlooks Panama Bay, near the present American Embassy. The Monument is carved from white marble and consists of four figures representing the four races. The figures hold up a globe with a statue of Vasco Núñez de Balboa, acclaimed discoverer of the Pacific Ocean.

BALDADO. Tubercular.

BALSERIA. Annual festival among the Guaymí Indians in the Provinces of Chiriquí and Bocas del Toro. The name comes from the balsa, or light throwing spear that is used in ceremonial fights.

BALZA. A colorful gathering among the Guaymí Indian groups, the balza is a kind of dance-contest or tournament in which contestants, using a long curved stick, try to trip each other. This continues until only one contestant is left standing. In days past, elaborate red and blue dyes were used to paint the body for the balza, and even today the contestants daub their faces and chests with black. The contest is terminated with a ceremonial toast, and then the güayacán is danced.

BARAJUSTAR. The act of fleeing impetuously.

BARRA. A group of persons or an audience arranged by the organizing entity to give support to a speaker. A claque.

BARU. One of twelve distritos in the Province of Chiriquí.

Its cabecera is Puerto Armuelles.

BARU VOLCANO.   An active volcano and the highest point
    of elevation in the country; approximately 3, 478
    meters (11, 410 feet) high.   In the Province of
    Chiriquí.

BASTIMENTOS.   One of three distritos in the Province of
    Bocas del Toro.   Its cabecera is Bastimentos.

BASTIMENTOS.   Cabecera of the Bastimentos District.
    Population: 374.

BAYANO RIVER.   Longest river in the country; 205 kilo-
    meters (129 miles) long, draining an area of 4, 280
    square kilometers.   In the Province of Panama.

BELALCAZAR, Sebastián de, 1495-1551. Sailed with
    Pedrarias in 1514 on his expedition to colonize
    Panama.   Belalcázar, after playing an initial part
    in founding a colony in Panama, earned fame as an
    explorer in his own right by leading one of the many
    quests for El Dorado and carried out exploration in
    Peru and into present day Colombia.   A rival of
    Federmann and Quesada, he was ultimately made
    Governor of Popayán, the western area of modern
    Colombia, but was soon in trouble both with locals
    and with the Crown, and died before it was straighten-
    ed out.   His death came in 1551.

BERRIONDO.   A vulgarism used to describe a despicable
    person.

BIDLACK TREATY OF 1846.   A treaty negotiated by Tomás
    Cipriano de Mosquera, then President of New
    Granada-Colombia, with the United States which
    assured the passage of American citizens across the
    Isthmus of Panama in exchange for Washington's
    protection of the Isthmus from British incursions.

BIMBIN.   A wild song-bird.

BIOMBO.   A small sling-shot made by children, used pri-
    marily for shooting at birds or fruit.

BIRULI.   A type of small cane, used for building cages for
    birds or small animals.

BOCACHO. A person with some teeth missing. Also, a
glass or other container with a chipped edge.

BOCARACA. A very venomous, tree-dwelling serpent.

BOCAS DEL TORO. One of the nine provinces of Panama,
located in the northwest part of the nation. Bordered
by the Caribbean on the north; by the Province of
Chiriquí on the south; by the Province of Veraguas on
the south and east; and by the nation of Costa Rica
on the west. It has an area of 3, 459 sq. mi. and its
capital is the city of Bocas del Toro. The three
distritos and their respective cabeceras are: Bastimentos, Bastimentos; Bocas del Toro, Bocas del
Toro; Chiriquí Grande, Chiriquí Grande. Total population of the province, official estimate of 1969, is
43, 600. Economically, the province is noted for its
agricultural produce. The major products are bananas and cocoa.

BOCAS DEL TORO. One of three distritos in the Province
of Bocas del Toro. Its cabecera is Bocas del Toro.

BOCAS DEL TORO. Capital city of the Province of Bocas
del Toro and cabecera of the district of the same
name. It is the largest city and the focal point of
the largest settled area north of the Continental
Divide and west of Colón. It is the clearing house
for banana and cocoa plantations in the region and a
center for ocean and air travel. Its population was
2, 459 in 1960.

BOCONA. A type of four-string, native guitar with a high
tone.

BOCON. A person who talks too much. A "blabber-mouth."

BOLIVAR PLAZA. Although this small park has been known
as the Bolivar Plaza since July 25, 1883, it was not
until 1923 that a monument to that liberator was sug-
gested. Then, all of the countries of Latin America
subscribed to its erection. Rodolfo Chiari, then
President of the Republic, dedicated the monument on
June 22, 1926. This coincided with the first centen-
nial of the Amphicytonic Congress, called by Bolívar.

BOLLO. A cylinder of cornmeal dough, wrapped in sugar

cane leaves or in corn husks and cooked.   Ingredients
vary.   A tamal, or tamale.

BOLUNGO.   A variety of tailless chicken.

BONCHAO.   Derived from the English bunch, used to indicate a great quantity of people or things.

BONGO.   A small sailing vessel, made from the trunk of
a tree.

BOQUERON.   One of twelve distritos in the Province of
Chiriquí.   Its cabecera is Boquerón.

BOQUERON.   Cabecera of the Boquerón District.   Population: 518.

BOQUETE.   One of twelve distritos in the Province of
Chiriquí.   Its cabecera is Bajo Boquete.

BORDER DISPUTES   see   COTO REGION and THOMSON-
URRUTIA TREATY.

BORRIGUERO.   A small reptile, very agile and very easily
frightened.   A member of the lizard family.

BOYD, Aguilino.   Panamanian Ambassador to the United
Nations 1968- .

BOYD, Dr. Augusto S., 1879- .   Served as Vice-President
under President Juan Demóstenes Arosemena and,
upon the latter's death, assumed the Presidency for
the few remaining months of the presidential term
(December, 1939-October, 1940).

BOYD, Augusto Samuel, Jr.   Boyd, born in 1918, graduated
from Washington University (Washington, D. C.,) and
was an attaché at the embassy in Washington D. C.
in 1939.   He was special auditory comptroller
general in 1940, assistant administrative general of
customs from 1940-1941, and private secretary to
the President of the Republic beginning in 1941.   He
became a member of the provincial assembly
(Panama), in 1941.

BOYD, Federico.   A leading political figure and member of
the 1903 provisional junta of government which was

formed on the declaration of independence of Panama
from Colombia.

BRIDGE OF THE AMERICAS.   Located on the Pacific side
of the Isthmus, the Bridge of the Americas not only
connects both banks of the Panama Canal, but also
serves as a link to the Inter-American Highway, thus
uniting Panama City and the interior of the Republic.
Built at a cost of some $20 million, the bridge was
opened on October 12, 1962.

BUCHE.   Said of a person who likes to drink.   A sot,
drunkard.

BUCHI.   A wild man, or uncivilized person.   From the
English, bush man.

BUGABA.   One of twelve distritos in the Province of
Chiriquí.   Its cabecera is La Concepción.

BULLARENGUE.   A regional dance of the Darién, similar
to the tamborito, but more sensuous and moving.

BULLERENGUE   see BULLARENGUE.

BUNAU-VARILLA, Philippe.   An engineer of and agent for
the French Canal Company, who attempted to sell
the company's rights to the route and a considerable
amount of machinery to various European powers.
The United States, which had come to realize the
value of a canal during the Spanish-American War,
was increasing its navy and Theodore Roosevelt
became interested in Bunau-Varilla's proposition.
When the British conveniently cancelled the Clayton-
Bulwer Treaty of 1850, the U.S. then struck a
bargain to pay the French Canal Company $40 million
for its rights and properties.   The U.S., dealing
with President Marroquín of Colombia, agreed to pay
that country $10 million plus a rental of $250,000.
However, the Colombian Congress refused to ratify
the Hay-Herán Treaty, as it was known.   Bunau-
Varilla had persuaded a group of revolutionists that
they could count on the support of the U.S.   Thus,
with the support of the commander of the Colombian
garrison, they seized control of Panama City on
November 3, 1903, and declared the independence of
the Republic of Panama.   Bunau-Varilla was not only

instrumental in promoting the revolution, he also saw
to its financing. Three days later, the independence
was recognized by the U.S., and, on November 18,
the Hay-Bunau-Varilla Treaty was signed at Washington. Bunau-Varilla was named as Panama's official
representative in Washington and engineered the financial dealings of the U.S.-Panamanian-French Canal
Company triad. The Hay-Bunau-Varilla Treaty contained essentially the same elements of the Hay-Herán
Treaty which was abrogated upon the independence of
Panama from Colombia.

BUNDE. A regional ceremonial dance, generally performed
around Christmas season, typical of the Dariên.
Also, a fiesta, or happy gathering or occasion.

BUNEAU-VARILLA, Phillipe   see   BUNAU-VARILLA,
Philippe.

BUREO. A party with lively dancing and other diversions.

BURGOS, LAWS OF (1512). The first Spanish code of laws
concerned with the governing and instruction of native
Americans.

BURUNDANGA. Any appetizing snack, generally sweet,
which children of all ages eat at any time.

-C-

CABECERA. Governmental administrative center and capital
of a distrito.

CABELLITOS DE ANGEL. A home-made candy, prepared
with long, thin strips of green papaya, cooked in a
syrup.

CABILDO. The town government of Spanish America. The
term has been expanded to include the municipal
building.

CABRESTILLO. From cabestrillo. A long gold chain,
adorned with trinkets and a pendant brooch, commonly
worn with the national dress for women, the pollera.

CACHO. A horn, i.e., of an animal. Also, in some areas,

a short anecdote or joke.   Also, a dice cup.

CACIQUE.   A native chief or head man.

CACIQUE.   The smallest and most frail of a nesting of
   parakeets.

CACIQUISMO.   Bossism, or undue influence and autocratic
   power over a village, town, or local area level.
   Previously common throughout Latin America, the
   system is still known in certain areas and at virtually all levels of government.

CADENA CHATA.   A collar, formed of small, interlaced
   gold links, generally worn with the typical woman's
   dress, the pollera.

CAIMANEAR.   To prejudice or deceive someone in business
   dealings.   Also, to obtain a given thing through
   deceit, intrigue, or pressure.

CALOBRE.   One of eleven distritos in the Province of
   Veraguas.   Its cabecera is Calobre.

CALOBRE.   Cabecera of the Calobre District.   Population:
   423.

CALUNGO.   A person or animal devoid of all hair or
   feathers.

CAMAJAN.   Lazy, indolent.

CAMARON.   Payment for small, odd jobs.

CANAL ZONE   see   PANAMA CANAL ZONE.

CAÑAÑA.   Force, energy, valor.

CAÑAZA.   Bamboo.

CAÑAZAS.   One of eleven distritos in the Province of
   Veraguas.   Its cabecera is Cañazas.

CAÑAZAS.   Cabecera of the Cañazas District.   Population:
   922.

CANCANEAR.   To read badly, or speak poorly, to stutter

or stammer.

CANCANELA   see   CAPISUCIA.   Word used in Los Santos
     region.

CANDELILLA.   A small ant, deep red in color, noted for
     its sharp, disagreeable bite.

CANILLA.   Refers to a thin leg, "spindle-shanks. "

CANYAC.   Popular name for marijuana or for hierba santa,
     a type of tropical opiate.

CAO.   A nocturnal bird, so called owing to its peculiar cry.

CAPACHO.   A bird, the goat-sucker, churn-owl.

CAPIRA.   One of ten distritos in the Province of Panama.
     Its cabecera is Capira.

CAPIRA.   Cabecera of the Capira District.   Population:
     642.

CAPISUCIA.   A wild bird, greyish in color, with a very
     pleasant song.

CAPITULACION.   A royal license contracted between the
     Spanish crown and a conquistador.   In return for the
     expense of conquest, financed privately, the con-
     quistador could take profits from the conquered
     land, extract labor, appoint municipal officers for
     the first year, and recruit soldiers and settlers.
     The crown received a fifth of the treasures taken or
     profits made.

CAPTAIN GENERAL.   The office was more that of a provin-
     cial viceroy, with as much autonomy as a viceroy
     and with direct responsibility to the Council of the
     Indies.   An exception, however, was in cases requir-
     ing important policy decisions, when the viceroy
     would be consulted.

CARA E CABALLO.   A medium-size, two-masted sailing
     vessel, made from a single tree trunk, larger than
     the bongo, with a small covering for protection from
     the elements.

CARACUCHA. A bush bearing flowers of the same name, pretty and very fragrant.

CARIBS. A rather loose term for groups of indigenes who inhabited the southern West Indies and the northern coast of South America, the Caribs made their way into the Isthmus at some as yet undetermined date. They evidently followed the coasts and rivers, ultimately making their way inland into what is modern Panama. By the fifteenth century they ruled those areas bordering the Caribbean Sea, which were then named after them. It is conceivable that had the Spaniards not arrived when they did, the Caribs, who were fierce and tenacious warriors, would have taken over the entire Isthmus.

CARNANZUELO. Fruit of the tree called espavé.

CARRICILLO. A thin, hollow, knotty, stemmed plant.

CARTUCHO. A paper bag of varying sizes, shapes and manufacture used in business. Also, a paper cone used by grocers.

CASA DE CONTRATACION. Often referred to as the Casa de las Indias, it was set up by the crown in 1503 to supervise commerce, navigation and emigration. It was subordinate to the Consejo de las Indias. In the eighteenth century, the policy of the Casa de Contratación was liberalized by the opening of new ports and the formation of more trading companies to stimulate trade. In Central America, all the legal traffic had to enter through Panama, Porto Bello, and Veracruz, with some limited west coast trade from Lima, Peru. The Casa was abolished in 1790.

CASA DE LAS INDIAS   see   CASA DE CONTRATACION.

CASCARAZO. A strong, dry blow, such as that given by a sheathed machete.

CASTILLA DEL ORO. In 1508, Diego de Nicuesa received a grant of land from Panama northward, called Veragua or, as it was hopefully renamed later, Castilla del Oro. In 1514 the area, centered in present-day Darién, came under the governorship of Pedro Arias de Avila (Pedrarias) and who brought

with him some 1500 colonists from Spain. Balboa had
temporarily ruled over the region in 1513. Pedrarias
soon moved across the Isthmus and founded Panama
on the Pacific side, the first Spanish settlement on the
Pacific Ocean (1519).

CASTILLERO REYES, Ernesto de Jesús. An educator and
historian, Castillero Reyes was born in Ocú, Panamá,
and attended the Seminario Conciliar de Panamá,
Instituto Nacional, receiving a teacher's certificate
in 1913. Beginning in 1929, he taught at the Colegio
de Artes y Oficios, Escuela Normal de Institutoras,
and the Instituto Nacional. He was secretary of the
delegation to the Pan-American Conference, in
Montevideo in 1933, and president of the delegation
of the Panamanian pedagogical mission to Venezuela,
Puerto Rico and the Dominican Republic. He was
director of the Biblioteca Nacional and author of many
works including Documentos históricos sobre la
independencia del istmo de Panamá (1930).

CASTILLO, MOISES, 1899- . A Nativist writer, Castillo
wrote poetry which evinced his dislike of cosmopolitan
life and cultural influences brought to Panama by the
Canal.

CATRE. Indolent, brainless, lack of ability.

CAUDILLO. Leader. The term first referred to the leaders
at the provincial level who led the movement for
freedom. Because of social and political instability,
it now refers to the concentration of political authority
in the hands of one person. Caudillismo is the term
applied to movements of this nature.

CAYUCO. A small canoe, built from one tree trunk.
Propulsion is by paddles.

CAZO. A large, long-handled spoon used for stirring sugar
cane juice while cooking it down.

CERVERA, Dámaso Alejandro. Cervera was born in Panama
City in 1886. He received his LL. D. from the
Universidad de Colombia in 1911. He was a judge
in the upper court, under secretary of interior and
justice, member of the municipal council of Panama
City, secretary of agriculture and public works, and

of foreign relations, of interior and justice, and public education. He was a teacher of psychology at the Instituto Nacional and a professor in the Law School at the Universidad Nacional, and Escuela Libre de Derecho. In 1934 he became president of the Supreme Court and magistrate. He is the author of various articles in periodicals and reviews.

CHACARA. A bag used by country people to carry their provisions or other utensils. Made of vegetable fibers.

CHAFLE. Common name for dinner.

CHAGRES. One of five distritos in the Province of Colón. Its cabecera is Nuevo Chagres.

CHAGRES RIVER. The second longest river in the country; 193 kilometers (122 miles) long, draining an area of 2, 600 square kilometers, the Chagres is located in the Provinces of Panama and Colón. Perhaps its greatest claims to fame are the Gatun and Madden Dams, which form the lakes of the same names. These lakes serve as water supply and control for the Panama Canal and also afford some flood control.

CHALINA. A cape, or mantilla.

CHAME. One of ten distritos in the Province of Panama. Its cabecera is Chame.

CHAME. Cabecera of the Chame District. Population: 625.

CHANCE. A fractional part of a national lottery ticket. By extension, opportunity.

CHANCERO. A person selling national lottery tickets.

CHANGAME. A bird, thrush.

CHANGO. A medium-size bird which feeds on grains, especially rice. Considered highly prejudicial to crops.

CHANGUATAL. A muddy place, a bog.

CHANGUINOLA RIVER. Seventh longest river in the

country; 110 kilometers (69 miles) long, draining
an area of 2, 810 square kilometers. In the Province
of Bocas del Toro.

CHARRO. In bad taste, vulgar, shoddy.

CHATA. A large tick.

CHEPIGANA. One of two distritos in the Province of
    Darién. Its cabecera is La Palma.

CHEPO. One of ten distritos in the Province of Panama.
    Its cabecera is Chepo.

CHEPO. Cabecera of the Chepo District. Population:
    1, 303.

CHEPO RIVER   see BAYANO RIVER.

CHIARI, Roberto Francisco. In May, 1960, Dr. Roberto
    F. Chiari was elected president, succeeding Ernesto
    de la Guardia. A fairly conservative political figure,
    Chiari indicated that anti-American violence would
    no longer enjoy official sanction, and his attitude
    toward Washington was reasonable. He attempted to
    play down the nation's almost total obsession with the
    Canal and began a movement which is slowly gaining
    ground to establish a "national identity" outside the
    influence of the Canal. He was succeeded in office
    by Marco Aurelio Robles in 1964.

CHIARI, Rodolfo, 1870-1937. President of the Republic
    from 1924 until 1928, Chiari successfully quelled
    the famous San Blas (Cuna) Indian rebellion of 1925.
    He also dealt with the problem of negotiating a new
    treaty with the United States, which was to replace
    the Taft Treaty of 1904. The latter had been intended
    as a modus vivendi during the construction of the
    Canal and was abrogated on June 1, 1924. Although
    a new treaty was signed in 1926, it was never ra-
    tified by the Panamanian Congress owing primarily
    to Article XI (which provided that Panama would
    consider herself in a state of war whenever the U. S.
    became involved in hostilities) and also to the pro-
    posed cession of land in Colón. Further, ex-Presi-
    dent Porras had quarreled with Chiari and led an

effort against ratification. Chiari served out his term and was succeeded by the Liberal, Florencio Harmodio Arosemena in 1928.

CHIBCHAS. A people, possibly arriving from eastern Colombia, or perhaps indigenous to the Isthmus, who worked in gold. Included were the Comagres, the Chiriquís, the Coclés and other lesser groups. Together, they occupied virtually the entire area of what is today Panama.

CHICHA. An indigenous, corn-based liquor.

CHICHEME. A drink prepared by boiling unground corn in water, and adding sugar, milk, and other ingredients to it.

CHICHI. Applied to a recently born child.

CHIMAN. One of ten distritos in the Province of Panama. Its cabecera is Chimán.

CHIMAN. Cabecera of the Chimán District. Population: 442.

CHINCHE. A restless, vivacious person. Also, an exigent, fastidious person.

CHINCHORRA. A name given to the guitar.

CHINGO. A short dress or pants. Also, a small vessel made from a single tree trunk.

CHINGONGO. Chewing gum. From English.

CHIRICANO. A corn and honey bollo cooked en casserole.

CHIRIPAZO. To hit on something by accident.

CHIRIQUI. One of the nine provinces of Panama, located in the southwest part of the nation. Bordered by the nation of Costa Rica on the west; by the Pacific Ocean on the south; by the Province of Bocas del Toro on the north; and by the Province of Veraguas on the east. It has an area of 3,381 sq. mi. and its capital is the city of David. The twelve distritos and their respective cabeceras are: David; Alanje,

Alanje; Boquete, Bajo Boquete; Boquerón, Boquerón;
Bugaba, La Concepción; Dolega, Dolega; Gualaca,
Gualaca; San Lorenzo, Horconcitos; San Félix, Las
Lajas; Barú, Puerto Armuelles; Remedios, Remedios;
Tolé, Tolé.   Total population of the Province, official
estimate of 1969, is 249,200.   In addition to cattle
raising, this province is noted for its sugar cane,
rice, bananas, cacao, and coffee.   Outside of Panama,
it is the most productive province in the nation.

CHIRIQUI GRANDE.   One of three distritos in the Province
of Bocas del Toro.   Its cabecera is Chiriqui Grande.

CHIRIQUI GRANDE.   Cabecera of the Chiriqui Grande District.   Population: 80.

CHIRIQUI VIEJO RIVER.   Eighth longest river in the country;
110 kilometers (69 miles) long, draining an area of
1,400 square kilometers.   In the Province of Chiriqui.

CHIRIQUI VOLCANO   see   BARU VOLCANO.

CHIRO.   Beach bird.   Also, the income from an odd job.

CHIROLA.   From chirona.   Jail.

CHITRA.   A small, bothersome insect fround on beaches.
Similar to sand fleas.

CHITRE.   One of seven distritos in the Province of Herrera.
Its cabecera is Chitré.

CHITRE.   Chitré, a city of 9,120 population, is the capital
city of the Province of Herrera and is the cabecera
of the Chitré District.   Located in the heart of a
fast-growing agricultural district, it is a market center for livestock and has cold-storage facilities, rice
warehouses, a corn mill, and many rice mills.   It
has a port on the Gulf of Panama, and with the exception of David, is'the only city in the interior with
modern shops.

CHIVA.   A collective transport vehicle.   Like a small bus
with seats along the sides.   Probably from Chevrolet.

CHIVERO.   Driver of a chiva.

CHOCAO. A dish prepared with ripe plantains or quineos
(a short banana), cooked with ginger. Coconut milk
is added to the mixture when eaten.

CHOCO INDIANS. A separate "tribe" of Indians which remains essentially isolated from the effective national
life of Panama, the Chocó inhabit the Province of
Darién in Panama. They have been described as blue-
eyed pygmies still sunk in aboriginal barbarism. Only
in the past decade has any progress been made in including them in the national scene. The Bayano River
hydroelectric project and the planned extension of the
Pan American Highway through the Darién will do
more to acculturate this group and, unfortunately, to
destroy their identity than any other acts during over
500 years.

CHOGORRO. A species of fresh water fish.

CHOMPA. An article of male clothing, similar to a quaya-
bera, a pleated shirt worn outside the trousers, mod-
erately decorated with buttons.

CHOROTECA see CAPISUCIA. Word used in Coclé region.

CHUCUNAQUE RIVER. Third longest river in the country;
172 kilometers (108 miles) long, draining an area of
5, 010 square kilometers. In the Province of Darién.

CHUECO. Incomplete, nonserviceable.

CHUIO. A bird with dark plumage, whose name is taken
from its song.

CHUMICO. A medium-size bush, with twisted trunk and
branches, with heavy leaves which are used for wash-
ing or polishing items, especially wood.

CHUNCHO. An old car, a "crate. "

CHUSPA. A lattice-work bag, used by rural peoples, made
from the cured skin of bull testicles.

CIMARRON. A type of bootleg liquor produced illegally in
clandestine stills, generally in the country.

CINCHO. A wooden mold used in the production of cheeses.

Also, a type of cinch used to break animals.

CINCO DE MAYO PLAZA. The "5th of May" Plaza contains
   an obelisk honoring the firemen who died when fire
   caused an explosion of the powder magazine in Panama
   City on May 5, 1914. It is best known as a parking
   place for the neighborhood.

CLAYTON-BULWER TREATY. Owing to rivalry between
   Great Britain and the United States, those two nations
   in 1850 negotiated the Clayton-Bulwer Treaty which
   provided that neither nation was to seek exclusive control over any part of Central America. Specifically
   exempted from the treaty was the Mosquito Indian pro-
   tectorate claimed by England. The treaty was nulli-
   fied by the Hay-Pounceforte Treaty in 1901.

COBRE RIVER. Tenth longest river in the country; 90 kilometers (57 miles) long, draining an area of 935
   square kilometers. In the Province of Veraguas.

COCLE. One of the nine provinces of Panama, located in
   the central part of the nation. Bordered by the Gulf
   of Panama on the south; by the Province of Veraguas
   on the west; by the Province of Colón on the north;
   and by the Province of Panama on the east. It has
   an area of 1,944 sq. mi. and its capital is the city
   of Penonomé. The six distritos and their respective
   cabeceras are: Penonomé, Penonomé; Aguadulce,
   Aguadulce; Antón, Antón; Natá, Natá; Olá, Olá; La
   Pintada, La Pintada. Total population of the Province, official estimate of 1969, is 118,000. This
   province is noted for agricultural produce, livestock,
   and the pre-Columbian archaeology found near Penonomé.

COCOBOLO. A bald-headed person, or one with the hair
   cut or shaved very short.

COCORITO. A small owl, with a strident, disagreeable cry.

COCORRON. An insect of the cicada family.

COLIN. Machete. A name given to all machetes in general
   by the country people, the name coming from the
   Collins cutlery firm in the United States.

COLOMBIA.   For 82 years, Panama was a part of Colombia,
     by whatever name.   From 1821 until Independence in
     1903, Panama made progress in virtually no way, ac-
     cording to the popular thinking of Panamanians.
     There is no doubt that there were fluctuations in the
     commercial and social climate of Panama while it was
     under the rule of Bogotá.   Latent animosity is still
     to be found, particularly among the elders of both na-
     tions, concerning the interrelationships of the two re-
     publics.

COLON.   One of five distritos in the Province of Colón.   Its
     cabecera is Colón.

COLON.   One of the nine provinces of Panama, located in
     the north-central part of the nation.   Bordered by the
     Caribbean on the north; the Province of Veraguas on
     the west; the Provinces of Coclé and Panama on the
     south; and the Comarca of San Blas on the east.
     Colón is divided into two sections by the Panama
     Canal.   It has an area of 2,879 sq. mi. and its capi-
     tal is the city of Colón.   The five distritos and their
     respective cabeceras are: Colón, Colón; Donoso,
     Miguel de la Borda; Chagres, Nuevo Chagres; Santa
     Isabel, Palenque; Portobelo, Portobelo.   Total popu-
     lation of the province, official estimate of 1969, is
     120,500.   The second largest distribution and market
     center of the nation is located in the capital of this
     distrito.   The Free Zone and subsidiary income from
     the Canal, along with some tourism are the backbone
     of local economy.   Agriculture is also an economic
     factor.

COLON.   Colón is the capital city of the Province of Colón
     and is the cabecera of the district of the same name.
     Founded as a result of the 1849 gold rush in Califor-
     nia, Colón sprang into existence under the name of
     Aspinwall in 1852 as the starting point for the Panama
     Railway.   The name was later changed to Colón at
     the insistence of the Panamanians.   Today Colón is
     Panama's leading Atlantic port and gateway to the
     Canal, and is the nation's second largest distribution
     and market center.   An extremely cosmopolitan port,
     one can see craft ranging from navy transport ships
     to banana boats to Cuna Indian dugout canoes lining
     the wharves.   The city is well provided with most
     modern conveniences and has become an important

distribution center for Latin American trade, especially since the inauguration in 1953 of the Colón International Free Trade Zone.   Its reported population in
1960 was 59, 598.

COLUMBUS, Christopher, 1451(?)-1506.   Famous Italian
explorer who, financed by Spain, founded the short-
lived town of Santa María de Belén on the Isthmus of
Panama in 1503.   This settlement was made during
Columbus' fourth and last voyage to the New World.

COMARCA.   A political division not yet having achieved
statehood; a territory.

COMARCA DE SAN BLAS.   A formal Territory of Panama,
San Blas is commonly lumped with the Colón Province
for statistical purposes.   It has an area of 3, 206
square kilometers, with a total of 19, 160 inhabitants
(1967).   The majority of the population is comprised
of Cuna Indians and related indigenous groups.   Agriculture and fishing are of major import to the economy, although tourism has become more significant
in the past two decades.   The Cuna Indians, for example, have opened some of their area in the San
Blas Islands to outsiders.

COMER.   To win points in a game.

CONCHUELA.   A type of clam, large and edible.

CONGO.   A type of wasp.   Also, their nest.

CONGRESS OF PANAMA (1826)   see   PANAMA CONFER-
ENCE (1826).

CONQUISTADOR.   Conqueror.   Name given to the Spaniards
who took part in the expeditions of conquest in the
New World.

CONSTITUTION.   The nation of Panama functions under the
Constitution adopted in 1946, although as of this writing various of the Constitutional guarantees are void
owing to the coup d'etat in October, 1968.   The Constitution of 1946, the third one in the country's history, establishes Panama as a centralized democracy,
provides for universal, direct, equal, and secret suf-
frage and divides the Government into executive, leg-

islative, and judicial branches. There are guarantees
of civil liberties similar to the first 10 amendments to
the Constitution of the United States. The President
is elected by direct popular vote for a 4-year term,
and at the same time a First and Second Vice President are chosen. The President may not be reelected
for the two terms immediately following his incumben-
cy. His Cabinet consists of eight ministers and the
heads of 15 autonomous Government agencies. Provincial governors serve at the pleasure of the executive.
The legislative organ is a unicameral National Assembly which has 42 members. The Assembly is in re-
cess about 8 months of the year and its functions are
exercised by a Permanent Legislative Commission of
seven principal members elected by the Assembly
prior to adjournments.

COPON. Applied to situations in which things have reached
an intolerable state.

COPOTE see COPON.

COQUILLO. A type of thick-stemmed bush which, when
slashed or cut, gives out a whitish, astringent liquid.

COQUITO. A white cloth, decorated with embroidered flowers, widely used in making the national woman's dress,
the pollera.

CORDILLERA CENTRAL see CORDILLERA DE TALA-
MANCA.

CORDILLERA DE SAN BLAS. An 8- to 10-mile wide Caribbean coastal mountain range, low (to 3,600 feet) and
gently contoured.

CORDILLERA DE TALAMANCA. A 20- to 35-mile wide belt
of volcanic mountains in western Panama, an extension of mountains of the same name in Costa Rica.
The highest peak is Barú.

CORONADO, Francisco de, 1510-1554. Sailed with Pedrarias in 1514 on his expedition to colonize Panama.
Coronado became famous in his own right by later
moving to New Spain, being commissioned by the viceroy to seize the land surrounding the fabled Seven
Cities of Cíbola and, in 1540, heading an expedition

of 270 Spaniards and some 900 Indians for the purpose. For nearly two years he searched for a land
of riches and passed through the present states of
New Mexico, Arizona, Texas, Oklahoma, and Kansas,
returning to Mexico in 1542.

COROTU. A very leafy tree with large trunks, generally
not too tall. It is generally used as a shade tree,
commonly for livestock.

CORREGIDOR. Nominally a local official with both judicial
and administrative powers in Spanish America, there
came to be two types of corregidor; the corregidor
for Spaniards who was a true autocrat unless curbed
by the Viceroy, and the corregidor for Indians who
saw to the collection of tributes and to labor drafts.
Until 1678 most corregidores were named by the viceroy, but then the Council of Indies took over their
appointment, possibly because it could sell the positions. These officials were generally despots in office and probably formed the basis of the future bossism or caciquismo.

COSITA. A snack or refreshment, generally for children,
taken in the afternoon hours.

COSTA RICA see COTO REGION.

COTO REGION. An area in southern-most Costa Rica which,
in 1921, became the focal point of a long-disputed
boundary disagreement between Panama and Costa Rica.
Previously subject to an arbitral award handed down
by the President of France in 1900 and redecided by
Chief Justice White of the U. S. Supreme Court in
1914, in favor of Costa Rica, the Panamanian government refused to honor the arbitration. In 1921, Costa
Rica attempted to occupy the region, but was defeated
by Panama. The United States intervened at that
point, and some months later insisted that Costa Rica
be permitted to occupy the Coto region without resist-
ance.

COTON. A rough cotton work shirt. From the English,
cotton.

CRISTOBAL. Capital of the Cristóbal District of the Canal
Zone, Cristóbal has a population of 817. Adjacent to

Colón, in the Republic, Cristóbal is at the Caribbean terminus of the Canal and many of the important shipping companies from throughout the world maintain offices here. Nine miles southwest of Cristóbal is Fort San Lorenzo, a reconstructed Spanish fort that was built by the Spanish conquistadores to defend the mouth of the Chagres River. Just over a mile to the south of Cristóbal may be seen the remains of a portion of the French Canal begun by de Lesseps.

CUACO. Pelican.

CUCUAS. In the Corpus Christi festival, a group of dancers. Also the name of the costume or disguise that is worn. The name is taken from the name of a tree. The bark of this tree is used to make up the dance costume.

CUCURUCHO. A shack or hovel.

CUIPO. A very tall tree, producing a light-weight wood, widely used in industry.

CUJI. A trap or deception.

CUMBIA. A popular Panamanian dance with a variety of music, execution, instruments, and steps.

CUNA INDIANS. Inhabitants of the San Blas Islands and adjacent lands on the Atlantic shores, the Cuna Indians hold themselves aloof from the remainder of the nation. The group, which lives much as their ancestors did five hundred or a thousand years ago, occupy some 50 of the approximately 400 atolls composing the San Blas Islands. From the time of Batidas in 1500, various efforts have been made to colonize the San Blas Islands, but it was not until 1913 that the first break through the wall of isolation occurred as two protestant missionaries set up shop at the invitation of the Indians. Subsequent hostilities and an open rebellion in 1925 led to no further incursions for many years although the Cuna men soon began to leave the islands for work. No truly effective "outside" incursion came until in the 1950's and especially the 1960's, when schools, an administrative center, a hospital, and some tourist facilities were established. Famous for their needlework and wood-carving, the

Cuna now carry on an active trade with visiting tour-
ists.

CURACHA. A typical Panamanian dance.

-D-

DAMA DE NOCHE. A parasitic plant of the orchid family.
Noted for the delicate, agreeable aroma it gives off
at night.

DARIEN. One of the nine provinces of Panama, located in
the southeast part of the nation   Bordered by the nation of Colombia on the east and southeast; by the
Gulf of Panama on the west and southwest; by the
Province of Panama on the west and northwest; and
by the Comarca of San Blas on the north and north-
east. It has an area of 6,488 sq. mi. and its capital is the city of La Palma. The two distritos and
their respective cabeceras are: Chepigana, La Palma;
Pinogana, El Real. Total population of the Province,
official estimate of 1969, is 24,800. This province,
though one of the more remote and backward ones today, is the site of important developments in the history of Panama, particularly since 1513, in which
year Balboa established a colony in the northeastern
portion of the region. Among the country's greatest
assets are the virgin forests of Darién, which contain
cabinet, dye, and building woods. The lack of transportation in the region has, however, kept the area
relatively untapped, commercially.

DAVID. One of twelve distritos in the Province of Chiriquí.
Its cabecera is David.

DAVID. Located some 308 miles west of Panama City, at
the extreme western end of the nation, David is the
Capital of the Province of Chiriquí and the cabecera
of the District of David. The population in 1960 was
22,924. The city was founded in colonial times, but
has kept pace with all progress and is today the commercial center for all of Chiriquí Province. It is
the clearing center for sugar cane, rice, bananas,
cacao, and coffee and boasts tanneries, distilleries,
soap factories, rice mills, an abattoir and meat-pack-
ing plant. It is an important stopover for truckers,

both intra- and international, and its airport is rated as an international port of entry. David is also a railhead and serves as a collection center for coastwise shipping of mother-of-pearl, tortoise shell, and wild animal skins. The Chiriquí Land Company, the owner and operator of large, scientifically run plantations, centers here and the United Fruit Company ships bananas from here. The traditional colorful public market is particularly interesting, and one architectural oddity is the old San José Church, which has a bell tower completely separate from the church. The tower was built separately, as a defense against hostile Indians during the settlement period.

DECLARATION OF PANAMA (1939). Perhaps the most important result of a meeting of representatives of all of the American Republics, held in Panama (September 23, 1939), was the Declaration of Panama which affirmed that "the American Republics, so long as they maintain their neutrality, are... entitled to have those waters adjacent to the American Continent... free from the commission of any hostile act by any non-American belligerent nation...." The principle thus laid down did, it is felt, discourage acts of war on the western side of the Atlantic during World War II.

DECLARATION OF PANAMA (1956). An American Presidents' Meeting of Panama was held in commemoration of the First Panama Congress held in 1826. The Declaration, signed by all of the presidents, set forth the political, economic, and financial principles of the American nations. A strengthening of the OAS was the end result of the Meeting and the Declaration.

DE LESSEPS, Ferdinand, 1805-1894. First famed for building the Suez Canal, de Lesseps headed the French Canal Company which was organized in 1879 for the purpose of building a sea-level canal across the Panamanian Isthmus. This plan, owing to physical and fiscal impracticability, was abandoned in favor of a lock canal. The company's resources, depleted by extravagance and gross mismanagement, were unequal to the task. Yellow fever, malaria, and other pestilence claimed so many lives that any further work was impossible. Although de Lesseps personally was not responsible, the company failed under scandalous

circumstances in 1889. A substantial amount of excavation was accomplished under his direction, and his engineering and personal abilities have never been under
serious question. The new company which took over the
rights and property had too little capital to carry on any
work of real significance and the Canal stagnated until
the purchase of the rights and equipment by the United
States in 1903. Following the collapse of the French
Canal Company, the prisons of Paris were soon abound-
ing with participants in the fiasco. It was too heavy a
blow for de Lesseps and he lost his reason, dying an
emotionally broken man.

DELGADILLO, Luis A. Born in Managua, Nicaragua, in 1887,
Delgadillo was a pianist, composer, and conductor.
Following his studies at the Universidad Nacional and
at the Royal Conservatory, Milan, Italy, he directed the
Banda de los Supremos Poderes, Managua, and was
teacher of music in schools from 1912-1921. He also
taught at the Conservatorio Nacional de Mexico from
1921-1925, and at the Conservatorio Nacional de Panamá
from 1943 on. He is the author of 400 songs and classical compositions and was a musical critic for many
years.

DESCACHALANDRADO. Sloppiness in dress and/or personal
hygiene.

DESECHO. A foot path, or narrow, little used trail.

DE SOTO, Hernando, 1500-1542. Sailed with Pedrarias in 1514
to aid in colonizing Panama. Earned fame in his own
right by his exploration and conquering in Peru where,
in November, 1533, he took Cuzco. Still later, on May
25, 1539, De Soto landed at or near present-day Tampa
Bay with about six hundred men and 223 horses, searching for riches and the key to the mysterious northland.
He and his men wandered through the southeastern and
south central states of the modern United States, going
as far west as Oklahoma. They found no wealth of any
consequence and De Soto died on May 21, 1542. He is
generally credited with the discovery of the Mississippi
River. Following his death, Luis de Moscoso led his
followers back down the river and ultimately reached
Mexico in 1543.

DIABLO FUERTE. A coarse, resistent cloth used for making

work pants.

DISTRITO. Governmental division of a province, approximately
akin to a county or parrish.

DOLEGA. One of twelve distritos in the Province of Chiriquí.
Its cabecera is Dolega.

DOLEGA. Cabecera of the Dolega District. Population: 728.

DOMINGUEZ ALBA, Bernardo, 1904- . Writing under the pen
name Rogelio Sinán, Domínguez is the author of short
stories, novels, and poetry. An example of each is:
Todo un conflicto de sangre (1946); Plenilunio (1947);
and Semana Santa en la niebla (1949).

DONOSO. One of five distritos in the Province of Colón. Its
cabecera is Miguel de la Borda.

DORACES. An Indian group from the Province of Chiriquí.

DORMILONAS. A type of earring worn with the pollera, in the
form of an arch, with small, pendant gold platelets.

DRAKE, Francis, 1540-1596. A British privateer, best known
in Panama for his sacking of Nombre de Dios in 1572,
and Panama in 1573. By far the most famous, or infamous, of Elizabeth's freebooters, Drake planned the
capture of the annual accumulation of silver at Nombre
de Dios for some three years, beginning in 1570. He
accomplished his end in the years mentioned, although
he missed the bulk of the silver shipment at Panama--
it was already on ships in the harbor. He went on to
further exploits, circumnavigated the globe, and finally,
in 1595, assembled a force of some 2,500 men for the
purpose of seizing all of Panama and making it his base
from which to conquer Peru. The Spaniards, however,
were much better prepared by this time and, aided and
abetted by disease and chiggers, they defeated his
forces. Drake died during the enterprise.

DUQUE, Tomás Gabriel. Born in 1890 in Panama City, Duque
received his formal education at Worral Hall Military
Academy, Peekskill, New York. He was director of the
newspaper La Estrella de Panamá from 1914-1932 and
of the Star and Herald from 1914- . He was deputy,
vice-president of the national assembly in 1924, and

secretary of agriculture and public works in 1924. He
was Vice-President of the Republic of Panama, and
provisional President (Oct. 1928), as well as secretary
of finance, 1928-30.

DURO.   Frozen cubes of flavored water, milk, etc.

                                -E-

ECONOMY.   Almost since its inception as an independent na-
        tion, Panama has been plagued with a persevering eco-
        nomic problem--an almost totally dichotomized econo-
        mic system. Actually, Panama has two distinct eco-
        nomic systems. On the one hand, there is the highly
        commercialized, highly sophisticated, service-oriented,
        urban economy of the two "Canal Cities, " Panama City
        and Colón. On the other hand, there is the remainder of
        the country, with few exceptions, which is oriented en-
        tirely to an agricultural rural economy. Her agricultur-
        al economy limps along with limited resources being
        applied to improve livestock raising and farming, while
        her agriculture is unable to feed the nation. While the
        nation is attempting to diversify somewhat and expand
        light industry and processing plants for products trans-
        shipped through the nation, there is not enough invested
        capital and even fewer resources to develop the needed
        technological programs needed for the industrial devel-
        opment desired. The major source of revenue, and one
        which is not popular in Panama, is the rent and payment
        for services associated with the functioning of the Pana-
        ma Canal.

EL MULATO see URRIOLA, José Dolores.

EL PORVENIR.   Cabecera of the Comarca de San Blas. Popu-
        lation: 54. The static population of El Porvenir is no
        indication of its activity. Located on a small islet of
        the same name, the village provides all types of aquatic
        recreation for tourists who fly into a short, sand strip.
        Fishing, boating, swimming, sightseeing by boat or
        canoe, water skiing and scuba diving, plus visits to the
        Cuna Indians on and around the island make this para-
        dise most attractive to Panamanians and foreigners
        alike.

EL REAL.   Cabecera of the Pinogana District. Population: 869.

EMPELUCHAR. To better, to recover from an illness.

EMPOLLERADA. A woman dressed in the pollera.

ENCHOCLAR. To close in, lock up, keep apart.

ENCISO. Lawyer (around 1510) left by de Ojeda as representative.

ENCOMIENDA. As originally instituted by the Spaniards on Hispaniola, the encomienda simply meant that each Spaniard strong enough to make himself respected would be placed in charge of a certain number of native charges. It grew to be a system of slavery or feudalism at its depth. Through this method of forced labor, the encomendero, who was nominally charged with the responsibility of Christianizing the natives put under his care, could exact labor or payment in kind from all of his serfs. The New Laws in 1542 attempted to correct some of the gross conditions, but the encomenderos successfully blocked their efficacy. Finally, a royal decree in 1720 set up a chain of phasing out the encomienda system and by the closing days of the Colonial Era, the encomienda had all but disappeared.

ENCUCURUCHARSE. To hide oneself.

ENGRILLARSE. To go into debt.

ENGUACAR. To keep green fruit or vegetables in a covered place for ripening purposes.

ENJARMA. A leather or wood apparatus hung over the withers of a horse or other animal for hauling cargo. Like a pack saddle.

ENSUEÑO. Greenery used in decorating bouquets of flowers.

ENTRE CHIVO Y CONEJO. In answer to the salutation "How are you?", this expression means approximately "more or less well."

ENTUMISION. To be as if paralyzed. Used in the area of Los Santos.

ENYUCADO. A dish prepared with yucca, milk, anise, and cloves.

ESCOBAR, Federico, 1861-1912. A poet of great merit.

ESPAVE. A very tall, straight tree with branches only at the top, whose wood is very light in weight and is used, among other things, for boat building.

ESPIRITU SANTO, Tomás del, 1834-1862. A classical poet of Panama.

ETHNOLOGY. For brief discussion, see ARCHAEOLOGY.

-F-

FACULTO. Capable, dextrous. Used by the farming class.

FAJINA. Work of one day's duration performed by a day-labourer in order to pay his annual tax.

FALTO. Ignorant, brainless, an idiot.

FAMILIAR. A black doll, symbol of the family demon or spirit, to which popular superstition attributes a certain power to the good of its owner.

FARACHO. A sudden, more or less serious seizure or attack of illness.

FARAGUA. The name of a certain grass used for livestock feed.

FARRA. A revel, spree, "toot, " or "blast. "

FICHA. A person with mean or evil ancestors.

FIRIFIRI. Extremely thin, cadaverous.

FLAG, PANAMANIAN. The Panamanian flag is divided into four quarters, with the upper one nearest the staff white in color with a blue star in its center; the outer one is red; the lower quarter next to the staff is blue; and the fourth, white with a red star in its center. It was officially adopted in 1903. The flag was designed in 1903 by the son of the first President of Panama. White stands for peace, red and blue for the two political parties existing at the time of independence, and the stars symbolize faith and strength.

FLAT ARCH. Famous for its role in proving the lack of earth-
quakes in Panama, paving the way for the Canal. In
1673, the Religious Order of Dominics began construction of a new convent on a plot within the then new city.
Fire destroyed the structure in 1671, leaving only part
of the church and chapel. To the left of that church is
the Flat Arch, 50 feet long and 35 feet wide, which was
built for the choir, and which contributed in a positive
way to the construction of the Canal, for by standing un-
supported for so long, it proved that the country was
free of tremors.

FOGAJE. Heat

FONTEYN, Dame Margot, b. 1919. An illustrious ballerina,
perhaps Panama's outstanding performer of the dance
for many years. Achieved unwanted publicity during
comic-opera activities of her husband (Sr. Arias) who,
while trying to raise a revolution against the de la
Guardia government, succeeded (without intent) in having his wife jailed for a night during April, 1959.

FOTINGO. An old, worn-out car.

FREGADERA. Insistence in bothering or boring someone.

FRENCH CANAL COMPANY. The first serious effort to con-
struct a canal across the Isthmus began in 1879 with
the formation of the French Canal Company, a brain-
child of a French engineer, Bonaparte Wyse. Wyse
managed to interest Ferdinand de Lesseps, of Suez
Canal fame, in his plans for a sea-level canal and
agreed to head up the operation. In 1880, at La Boca,
de Lesseps' seven-year-old daughter, Fernanda,
inaugurated the work of excavation by turning the first
shovel of earth. However, the "Scandal of Panama, "
as the project came to be known, saw the squandering
of hundreds of millions of francs, with such items as
10, 000 snow shovels being purchased and sent to the
canal site; a company director inspecting the excavation
in a $40, 000 motor coach; the purchase of 15, 000
torches to illuminate the future, night-time inauguration of the canal; and new locomotives that were acci-
dentally derailed and abandoned to rust. Worried
stock-holders eventually understood the corruption that
existed and took their complaints to court, where a
subsequent investigation uncovered untold graft. The

company went into bankruptcy, the prisons of Paris
were soon full of the schemers who had been squandering their investors' money, and de Lesseps, although innocent of any wrong-doing, broke mentally,
never to recover his reason.   See PANAMA CANAL
for succeeding events.

FRENCH PLAZA.   The Plaza Francesa has had its name
since 1920 when a law was enacted to name it in
honor of the original constructors of the Canal.
The Government of Panama and nine other nations
paid $30,000 for the monument honoring the French
engineers.   There is also an obelisk dedicated
December 4, 1923, under which a document contain-
ing the signatures of 5,000 officials and dignitaries
was placed.

FRONTERIZO see ADELANTADO.

-G-

GAILLARD, Col. David.   Gaillard Cut in the Panama Canal
is named after Col. Gaillard who was in charge of
this part of the Canal excavation until his death in
1913.

GAILLARD CUT.   The deepest excavations for the Canal
were made through the section called Gaillard Cut.
The banks exceed 300 feet in height in some areas,
passing through the Continental Divide.   It is about
9 miles long and it was in the "Cut" that the mas-
sive slides occurred which have closed the Canal on
five occasions.   In the cut is found the spectacular
view often seen in classic photos of the Canal.

GALIMANY, Alberto.   Galimany was born in Panama City
in 1889.   He studied at the Conservatorio de Música,
Barcelona, Spain.   He directed the Banda Republi-
cana de Panamá from 1912-1937 and was teacher of
music in schools, and an orchestra conductor.   He
has written numerous musical compositions.

GAMONAL.   A cacique, or local political head.

GARAY, Narciso, 1876- .   Panamanian Ambassador to the
Organization of American States, 1968- .

GATUN LAKE.   Gatun Lake, with an area of about 164
    square miles, was for many years the largest arti-
    ficial lake in the world.   The Chagres River, the
    one indispensable key to the existence of the Panama
    Canal, was dammed to form Gatun Lake which has a
    mean elevation of 85 feet above sea-level.   The lake,
    which has a calculated deposit of 183 billion cubic
    feet of water, is held back by Gatun Dam which is
    1.5 miles long and a quarter of a mile wide, with a
    height of 103 feet above the Atlantic sea-level.

GENERAL DECLARATION OF NEUTRALITY (1939).   Adopted
    by a conference of representatives of the foreign
    ministers of all the American republics, held in Pan-
    ama September 23, 1939, the intent of the Declaration
    was for the American republics not to become in-
    volved in the growing European conflict.   While the
    vote was unanimous the intent was thwarted some
    two years later.

GOETHALS, Col. George W., 1858-1928.   An energetic,
    professional army man, Col. Goethals was named
    head of the Canal project after the U.S. had taken
    it over in 1903.   Under his capable, if somewhat se-
    vere command the project moved ahead steadily to
    completion in 1914.

GOLDEN CASTILE   see CASTILLA DEL ORO.

GOMA.   A hangover.

GONZALEZ DAVILA, Gil.   In 1522-23, under authority in-
    dependent of Pedrarias, he led a combined land-sea
    expedition westward from the Isthmus, conquered the
    area about the Gulf of Nicoya and Lake Nicaragua.

GOOD NEIGHBOR POLICY.   Growing out of good will inau-
    gurated by the Wilson administration, the "Good
    Neighbor Policy" was promulgated by Franklin Delano
    Roosevelt, beginning in 1933 with his pronouncements
    of the desire of the U.S. to act as a good neighbor
    to other American nations.   The policy was under-
    scored by Cordell Hull, then Secretary of State, at
    the Seventh Pan American Congress in Montevideo
    (1933) when he stated that this "Good Neighbor Poli-
    cy" was a part of the United States' official posture
    and that "... no government need fear any intervention

on the part of the United States...." This policy
led to the abrogation of the Platt Amendment in 1934,
the withdrawal of U. S. troops from Haiti and the
signing of a pact of non-intervention by the U. S. and
Panama.

GORGAS, Dr. Wm. C., 1854-1920. A professional army
officer, Dr. Gorgas, working under the general command of Col. Goethals, supervised the extermination
of mosquitoes, and other health measures soon after
the U. S. took over the Canal project. It is owing
to Gorgas that yellow fever and malaria were eradi-
cated so swiftly and that other health measures were
effected which led to inestimable benefits for Panama
as well as for the inhabitants of the Zone.

GOVERNORS OF THE GRANADINE AND COLOMBIAN ERA.
(Dates indicate terms of office).
Carreño, José María (Military Governor), 1822-1826.
Icaza Arosemena, Carlos (interim), 1823.
Argote, Juan José (Civil Governor), 1822-1826.
Muñoz, Manuel (interim), 1826.
de Fábrega, José, 1826-1827, 1829-1830.
Espinar, José Domingo, 1827, 1830-1831.
Sardá, José, 1828-1829.
Alzuru, Juan Eligio, 1831.
Herrera, Tomás, 1831-1832.
Jiménez, Pedro, 1832.
Argote, Juan José, 1832-1833.
Feraud, Juan B., 1833-1834.
Hurtado, Manuel José, 1834-1836.
de Obarrio, Pedro, 1836-1840.
Icaza Arosemena, Carlos, 1840-1841, 1851, 1871,
1872.
Herrera, Tomás, 1841-1842, 1845-1846, 1849, 1851,
1852.
Chiari, Miguel, 1842.
Victoria y Echavarría, J., 1842.
Pineda, Anselmo, 1843-1845.
de Obaldía, José, 1845, 1850-1851, 1858-1860.
Quesada, Manuel, 1846.
Barriga, José María, 1846.
Díaz, Manuel María (interim), 1849, 1851, 1855,
1862-1863.
Bermúdez, Juan Antonio, 1851.
Planas, Antonio, 1852.
Arze De Mata, Bernardo, 1852, 1853 (interim), 1855.

Roldán, Salvador Camacho, 1852-1853.
Urrutia Añino, José María, 1854.
Echavarría, Juan, 1854-1855.
de Diego, Isidro, 1855.
Pacheco, Damián José, 1855.
Arosemena, Justo, 1855.
de Fábrega, Francisco, 1855-1856.
Calvo, Bartolomé, 1856-1858.
Gamboa, Ramón, 1858.
Núñez, Rafael (transitory), 1858-1859.
de la Guardia Arrue, Santiago, 1860-1862.
Goytía, Pedro, 1863.
Santacoloma, Peregrino, 1863-1864.
Calancha, José Leonardo, 1864-1865.
Colunje, Gil, 1865-1866.
Olarte Galindo, Vicente, 1866-1868.
Casanova, Remigio, 1868.
Díaz, Juan José, 1868, (interim) 1875.
Ponce, Fernando, 1868.
Correoso, Buenaventura, 1868-1871, 1871-1872,
    1876-1878.
Sosa, Julián, 1871.
Mendoza, Juan, 1871, 1872.
Neyra, Gabriel, 1872-1873, 1873-1874.
Cervera, Dámaso A., 1873, 1880-1883, 1883-1884,
    1885.
Vives León, José María, 1873, 1883, 1884-1885.
Pernet, Juan (transitory), 1873.
Miró, Gregorio, 1873-1875.
Arosemena, Pablo, 1875, 1885.
Camargo, Sergio, 1875.
Aizpuru, Rafael, 1875-1876, 1885.
Sasorla, José Ricardo, 1878-1879.
Ortega, Gerardo, 1879.
Ruiz, Benjamín, 1885.
Gónima, Carlos A., 1885.
Vila, Ramón Santodomingo, 1885-1886.
Montoya, Miguel, 1886.
Meynar, Carlos, 1886.
Amador Guerrero, Manuel, 1886.
Posada, Alejandro, 1886-1887, 1888.
Aycardi, Juan V., 1887-1888, 1888-1893.
Arango, Ricardo, 1893-1898.
Mutis Durán, Facundo, 1898-1899, 1903.
Orillac, Alejandro (transitory), 1899-1900.
Campo Serrano, José María, 1899-1900.
Albán, Carlos, 1900-1902.

Arjona, Aristides (accidental), 1902.
Salazar, Victor Manuel, 1902-1903.
de Obaldía, José Domingo, 1903.

GOYTIA, Victor Florencio.   Born in 1899, Goytia received
    an LL. B. from the University of Panama in 1920.
    He was 1st secretary of legation from 1924-1926, and
    secretary to President of the Republic in 1931.   He
    was also deputy of the Asamblea Nacional from 1932
    to 1936, and Minister of education, 1942-44.   He has
    authored several works.

GRANADINE CONFEDERATION.   In 1855, Panama became
    an autonomous state of the Granadine Confederation
    (Condereración Granadina) and later, in 1862, re-
    mained as a state in the United States of Colombia
    until independence in 1903.

GUACHARA.   A musical instrument similar to the güiro,
    an instrument made from a particular gourd.   The
    gourd is striated and a stick is scraped across the
    striations to make a rhythmic sound.

GUACHARACA.   A musical instrument like the maracas.
    A gourd into which rocks have been placed.   Shaken,
    it becomes a rhythm instrument.

GUACHIMAN.   A watchman.   From English, watchman.

GUACIMO.   A medium-size tree with yellow flowers whose
    pulp is used for making hawsers or whose wood is
    used for rustic building purposes.

GUACO.   From Quechua, a native burial in which personal
    adornment and/or jewels generally are put with the
    body.   Also, the objects found in such burials.
    Also, a hole in the ground for ripening green fruit.

GUACUCO.   A person of the Negro race.

GUALACA.   One of twelve distritos in the Province of
    Chiriquí.   Its cabecera is Gualaca.

GUALACA.   Cabecera of the Gualaca District.   Population:
    1, 387.

GUANDU.   Pole beans.

GUARACHO. A bird with black and white plumage, a sharp, cutting beak and feet somewhat like those of a chicken.

GUARAGUADO. Said of a person who is ungainly, uncouth, awkward, or ridiculous.

GUARARE. One of seven distritos in the Province of Los Santos. Its cabecera is Guararé.

GUARARE. Cabecera of the Guararé District. Population: 864.

GUARDIA, Ernesto de la, b. 1904. On May 13, 1956, de la Guardia, with the backing of the National Patriotic Coalition, was elected president and was inaugurated October 1 of that year. A new revision of the 1936 Canal Treaty had just been signed on January 25, 1955 and, earlier in that month, former President Remón had been assassinated. Things were somewhat chaotic. Dissatisfaction with inequality in payment of Panamanian workers vs. American workers in the Canal Zone led to strained diplomatic relations in 1959. Nationalists and, purportedly, Communist forces exploited the situation and a mob attempted to enter the Zone on November 3 in order to hoist the Panamanian flag. In a formal protest, Washington also declared itself ready to discuss the problems, most of which were engendered by supposed or real misinterpretations of the 1955 economic treaty. Another mob again attempted to enter the Zone on November 28, but were driven back by the Guardia Nacional on the orders of de la Guardia. Finally, by orders from Washington, the Panamanian flag was hoisted at one place within the Zone, and tempers cooled. The agitated rule of de la Guardia, who was not successful nor, perhaps, desirous, in quelling the foment, came to an end with the election of the relatively conservative Roberto Francisco Chiari in May 1960.

GUARDIA, Ricardo Adolfo de la, b. 1899. Ricardo A. de la Guardia was installed as President in October, 1941, when Arnulfo Arias who had shown inclinations to side with the Axis, or at best to maintain formal neutrality during World War II, left the country without permission from Congress. De la Guardia, who

had been the Minister of Government and Justice, had
his term extended by Congress to end in 1947. However, after affirming this act, the cabinet resigned,
the 1941 constitution was suspended, and the assembly
was dissolved. Members of the assembly met to pro-
claim J. B. Duncan as president under the Constitution of 1941. However, in June, 1945, a constituent
assembly elected Enrique A. Jiménez as provisional
president. De la Guardia essentially remained in office during all of the machinations. In 1946, the assembly adopted a new constitution, national elections
were held in May, 1948, and Domingo Díaz Arosemena was declared the winner and president.

GUARDIA NACIONAL. Panama's combined police force and
army.

GUARDIA Y AYALA, Victor de la, 1772-1824. Perhaps the
foremost author of his day, Guardia y Ayala's La
política del mundo, a tragedy in verse, was the first
dramatic work composed and performed in Panama.

GUATE. A very acid fruit which looks like a small squash.

GUAYACAN. A round dance performed almost exclusively
among the Guaymí Indian groups. This dance follows
the balza, a dance-contest.

GUAYMI INDIANS. An Indian tribe or group found generally
in the western mountains of mainland Panama.

GUAYUCO. A codpiece, made from a gourd, used by the
Cochó Indians.

GÜICHICHE. A type of wild duck.

GULF OF SAN MIGUEL. Site of Balboa's discovery of the
Pacific

GULF OF URABA. Today part of Colombia's territorial
waters, the Gulf was the site of de Ojeda's first
settlement of San Sebastián in 1508.

-H-

HAMAQUEAR. To give someone a good shaking.

HAY-BUNAU-VARILLA TREATY. Following the Colombian
    Congress' rejection of the Hay-Herrán Treaty, the
    people of Panama declared themselves independent on
    November 3, 1903. Independence was recognized by
    the U. S. three days later, and on November 18, the
    Hay-Bunau-Varilla Treaty was signed in Washington.
    This agreement gave the U. S. the right to build a canal
    across the Isthmus on a strip of land five miles wide
    on either side of the future canal granted in perpetuity,
    in return for $10 million plus an annuity of $250, 000.
    The U. S. agreed to guarantee Panama's freedom and
    assumed the task of maintaining law and order in that
    nation. The treaty has been revised many times, with
    the U. S. now paying in excess of $2 million dollars an-
    nually. At the time of this writing, a new treaty which
    would authorize a new, sea-level canal is being held in
    abeyance by both the Panamanian and U. S. Governments,
    and growing talk of the revival of a "third lock system, "
    promulgated in the 1940's, is heard.

HAY-HERRAN TREATY. A treaty concluded between Colombia
    and the United States in January, 1903. The treaty au-
    thorized the French Company to sell its canal rights to
    the U. S., gave the U. S. a zone ten kilometers wide for
    the canal, and gave Colombia $10 million plus an an-
    nuity of $250, 000 starting nine years after the rati-
    fication of the treaty. The Colombian Congress, how-
    ever refused to ratify the treaty, and this led to the
    revolt of Panama and its ultimate independence from
    Colombia.

HAY-PAUNCEFOTE TREATY. A treaty signed by the United
    States and Great Britain in 1901 which gave the U. S.
    the right to build a canal across the Isthmus. The
    Clayton-Bulwer Treaty of 1850 was abrogated.

HAYES, President Rutherford B., 1822-1893. President of
    the United States who, in futile opposition to the
    French Canal Company, had stated the position of the
    U. S. in 1880 as: "The policy of this country is a
    canal under American control. "

HERRERA. One of the nine provinces of Panama, located
    in the south central part of the nation. Bordered by
    the Province of Veraguas on the west and northwest;
    by the Province of Coclé on the north; by the Gulf of
    Panama on the east; and by the Province of Los

Santos on the south and southeast. It has an area of
937 sq. mi. and its capital is the city of Chitré.
The seven distritos and their respective cabeceras
are: Chitré, Chitré; Las Minas, Las Minas; Ocú,
Ocú; Parita, Parita; Pesé, Pesé; Los Pozos, Los
Pozos; Santa María, Santa María. Total population
of the province, official estimate of 1969, is 75,900.
Agriculture is the mainstay of this province.

HERRERA, Dario, 1870-1941. The earliest and a leading
figure in the modernismo movement in Panama,
Herrera was and is considered to be one of the best
of Panamanian poets. He was a close friend of
Rubén Darío, the famous Nicaraguan poet. He is
best known for his collection of short stories Horas
lejanas.

HERRERA, José de la Cruz. A teacher and a writer,
Herrera was born in 1876 in Garachiné, Panama.
He graduated from the Colegio Mayor de Nuestro
Señora del Rosario, in Bogotá, in 1899, and received
the degree professor of veterinary medicine from the
University of Bogotá in 1899. He was the author of
Apuntes sobre estética, Influencia del cristianismo
en la literatura española, and many others. He also
translated many works from the Greek.

HERRERA, Tomás, 1804-1854. In 1840, Herrera declared
the union (1832) between Panama and New Granada
at an end and led a revolution which accomplished
that aim. Until December 31, 1841, an independent
government, to which Herrera was party, ruled
the country which was named the Free State of the
Isthmus.

HICO. A name for the handle on the bag known as a chá-
cara. Also, the threads which are drawn together
at the ends of a hammock and used for hanging it.

HIERBA SANTA. A type of tropical opiate.

HORCONCITOS. Cabecera of the San Lorenzo District.
Population: 1,042.

HORQUETA PEAK. Sixth highest point of elevation in the
country; approximately 2,140 meters (7,019 feet)
high. In the Province of Chiriquí.

HUICHICHE see GÜICHICHE.

-I-

ILLUECA, ANA ISABEL, 1903- . Expressing a glorifica-
    tion of the traditional way of life, Illueca belongs
    among the Nativist poets.

INTERAMERICAN PEACE COMMITTEE. An outgrowth of
    one of the provisions of the Rio Treaty of 1947, the
    Interamerican Peace Committee (currently comprised
    of representatives from the United States, El Salva-
    dor, Mexico, Uruguay, and Venezuela) may act in
    any dispute between American nations, either uni-
    laterally or on the request of any government, but
    the consent of the disputing nations must be obtained
    prior to any investigation. Activated in 1959.

INTERNATIONAL COFFEE ORGANIZATION. Established in
    1958 at a meeting of all coffee-producing nations of
    the Western Hemisphere, the Organization, with
    Panama being one of the fifteen signatories to the
    enabling legislation, sees to the maintenance of the
    coffee policies agreed upon by the participating na-
    tions. The main aim of the Organization is produc-
    tion control and stabilization of coffee prices.

-J-

JABA. A basket of varying size and shape, made with
    interlaced reeds or cane.

JAMAQUEAR see HAMAQUEAR.

JERGA. A native dish prepared with beans, meats, and
    vegetables. A stew.

JIPIJAPA. A hat made from the fine, white fiber of the
    jipijapa palm. Made in Ecuador. Erroneously called
    a Panama Hat.

JUMA. A drunk, a brawl.

JUNTA. A rural "working bee" which serves a dual pur-
    pose as a social gathering. Also, and more com-

monly, an assembly or council, particularly a Spanish
or Latin American legislative or administrative body.

-K-

KORSI, Demetrio, 1899- . Technically a Nativist writer,
    Korsi was strongly affected by European writers. His
    first major work was El viento en la montaña (1926),
    while his later, more famous work Los gringos
    llegan y la cumbia se va decries the United States'
    influence on the native culture of Panama.

KUNAS see CUNAS.

-L-

LA CHORRERA.   One of ten distritos in the Province of
    Panama.   Its cabecera is La Chorrera.

LA CHORRERA.   Cabecera of the La Chorrera District,
    with a population of 8, 652, La Chorrera is noted
    for the El Chorro and Santa Rita Falls and for the
    recreation area above the falls.   The La Chorrera
    area is also known for its cattle, coffee, grain, and
    orange growing.   It is served by a small airport and
    is located just 10 miles west of Panama City.   On
    March 30, the Fiesta of St. Francis is held in com-
    memoration of the town being saved during the War
    of 1000 days (1899-1903), as a result of the women
    of the town praying to the patron for salvation of the
    city.

LA CONCEPCION.   Cabecera of the Bugaba District.   Popu-
    lation: 3, 063.

LA MESA.   One of eleven distritos in the Province of
    Veraguas.   Its cabecera is La Mesa.

LA MESA.   Cabecera of the La Mesa District.   Population:
    591.

LA PALMA.   Capital of the Province of Darién and cabecera
    of the Chepigana District, the town of La Palma had
    a population of 1, 885 in 1960.   It is best known as a
    starting place for hunts in the interior, expecially in

the hunting country to the southeast of the town.

LA PINTADA.   One of six distritos in the Province of
       Coclé.   Its cabecera is La Pintada.

LA PINTADA.   Cabecera of the La Pintada District.   Popu-
       lation: 491.

LA VILLA RIVER.   Ninth longest river in the country; 90
       kilometers (57 miles) long, draining an area of 1,200
       square kilometers.   In the Provinces of Herrera and
       Los Santos.

LADINO.   An Indian or Negro who speaks Spanish and, by
       extension, an acculturated or miscegenated Indian or
       Negro.

LAS LAJAS.   Cabecera of the San Félix District.   Popula-
       tion: 1,099.

LAS MINAS.   One of seven distritos in the Province of
       Herrera.   Its cabecera is Las Minas.   ·

LAS MINAS.   Cabecera of the Las Minas District.   Popula-
       tion: 494.

LAS PALMAS.   One of eleven distritos in the Province of
       Veraguas.   Its cabecera is Las Palmas.

LAS PALMAS.   Cabecera of the Las Palmas District.
       Population: 714.

LAS TABLAS.   One of seven distritos in the Province of
       Los Santos.   Its cabecera is Las Tablas.

LAS TABLAS.   Las Tablas is the Capital of the Province of
       Los Santos and is the cabecera of the Las Tablas
       District.   Its population in 1960 was 3,165.

LATIFUNDIO.   Large land holdings.   Large farms or
       ranches; large estates or plantations.   Traditionally
       in Panama and throughout Latin America, a minority
       of individuals or institutions have, from time to
       time, controlled the majority of the land.

LAVADA.   Insult, strong reprimand.

LEAGUE OF NATIONS. Because of her role in the First
     World War, Panama was entitled to participate in
     the Peace Conference. She signed the peace treaty
     and became a member of the League of Nations
     (1920).

LECHE. Used in the idiom "tener leche," it means, to be
     lucky.

LEFEVRE, Ernesto, b. 1907. Served as President of
     Panama, 1920-1924. Lefevre was duly elected and
     served his full term without any undue consequences
     or untoward happenings.

LEONCICO. Balboa's dog. It is said that Leoncico drew
     the pay of an army captain.

LEWIS, Roberto. Lewis was born in Panama City in 1874.
     A well-known painter, sculptor, and teacher, Lewis
     studied at the Collège La Salle and the Académie
     Nationale des Beaux Arts, Paris. He was a teacher
     of drawing at the Instituto Nacional, Escuela Normal,
     Escuela de Artes y Oficios and director of the Museo
     Nacional and Academia de Pintura, during the years
     1913-1938. His works include the ceiling, curtains
     and murals of the foyer, Teatro Nacional 1905-07,
     murals and gallery of portraits of presidents of the
     Republic in the Presidential Palace, etc.

LLANTA. A small, round roll made of grainy sweet dough,
     fried in oil.

LOPEZ, Carlos A. Minister of Foreign Affairs. Appointed
     to office by the Provisional Junta of Government in
     1968.

LOPEZ RUIZ, Sebastian, 1741-1823. A physician and nat-
     uralist who wrote monographs on Panamanian soci-
     ology. Considered as one of the first serious writ-
     ers of Panama.

LOS POZOS. One of seven distritos in the Province of
     Herrera. Its cabecera is Los Pozos.

LOS POZOS. Cabecera of the Los Pozos District. Popu-
     lation: 323.

LOS SANTOS.   One of seven distritos in the Province of Los
     Santos.   Its cabecera is Los Santos.

LOS SANTOS.   Cabecera of the Los Santos District.   Popu-
     lation: 2,608.

LOS SANTOS.   One of the nine provinces of Panama, located
     in the south central part of the nation.   Bordered by
     the Pacific Ocean on the south; by the Province of
     Veraguas on the west; by the Province of Herrera on
     the north and northwest; by the Gulf of Panama on the
     northeast and east.   It has an area of 1,482 sq. mi.
     and its capital is the city of Las Tablas.   The seven
     distritos and their respective cabeceras are: Las
     Tablas, Las Tablas; Guararé, Guararé; Los Santos,
     Los Santos; Macaracas, Macaracas; Pedasí, Pedasí;
     Pocrí, Pocrí; Tonosí, Tonosí.   Total population of
     the province, official estimate of 1969, is 81,800.

LUQUE, Hernando de.   Sailed with Pedrarias in 1514 on his
     expedition to colonize Panama.   De Luque, who was
     a priest, was instrumental in raising funds for the
     Conquest of Peru, and may be considered as a part-
     ner in that conquest, along with Francisco Pizarro
     and Diego de Almagro.   De Luque did not, however,
     live to see his partners' final triumph of conquest.

                              -M-

MACALLASO.   Worn out, spent, almost useless.

MACARACAS.   One of seven distritos in the Province of
     Los Santos.   Its cabecera is Macaracas.

MACARACAS.   Cabecera of the Macaracas District.   Popu-
     lation: 680.

MACHACANTE.   Applied to monetary units, e.g., the
     Balboa or the dollar.

MACHIGUA.   A name applied to the Indians in the Territory
     of San Blas.   The Cuna Indian.   In the Cuna lan-
     guage, machigua means "child."

MACUA.   A spell, or hex.

MADDEN LAKE. Formed by damming the Chagres River
    near the village of Alhajuela, Madden Lake is de-
    signed to augment the reserve water supply for ope-
    ration of the locks of the Panama Canal and for
    maintaining adequate navigational depth in the Canal.
    A secondary reason is hydroelectric power for the
    Canal operations and the dam is also instrumental in
    flood control.

MALARIA see GORGAS, Dr. Wm. C.

MANDUCO. A short, thick stick or club used for beating
    clothing when washing.

MAPANA. A very venemous snake of Panama. Also called
    a verrugosa.

MARIN, Chang, 1922- . Chosen as an example of the out-
    standing, younger poets of this age, Marín is a con-
    temporary poet and is recognized among the frater-
    nity as one of the better, if not the best, in Panama
    today.

MARROQUIN, José Manuel. Marroquín who, as Vice-Presi-
    dent of Colombia, had deposed President Sanclemente,
    was instrumental in the creation and signing of the
    Hay-Herrán Treaty, which was never ratified by his
    congress. It has often been suggested that he built
    the opposition of his congress in order to obtain
    more money from the U.S. for rights to dig the
    Canal and/or obtain certain other powers. Often
    considered a traitor of his country for his part in
    the "Panama Affair."

MATADO. A person without funds, broke.

MAYA. A highly developed civilization centering in lowland
    Yucatán and Guatemala, predating the Christian era.
    It is conjectured that the "stonecutters" of Panama
    were probably descendants of the Mayas, their incur-
    sion into Panama being pre-Columbian. These peo-
    ple occupied the occidental areas of the Isthmus.
    Much archaeologic work remains to be done concern-
    ing this purported Maya incursion.

MAYO. Diarrhea, especially that which comes on at the
    onset of the rainy season.

MECO. Name given to the Antillean Negro.

MEJENGUE. Force, vigor, energy.

MEJORANA. A type of five-string, native guitar similar to a standard, Spanish guitar.

MENDEZ PEREIRA, Octavio. Mendez Pereira was born in Aguadulce, Panamá in 1887. He graduated from the Universidad de Chile in 1913. He was a teacher at the Instituto Nacional and President from 1918-23 and also beginning in 1933. He became president of the Universidad de Panamá in 1935. He was a delegate to the League of Nations and International Labor Conference. He is the author of Historia de la literatura española (3d ed.), and the Historia de Ibero-América (1936), among others.

MENDOZA, Carlos Antonio. Served briefly (March-September, 1910) as temporary President of Panama subsequent to the death of José Domingo de Obaldía and prior to Pablo Arosemena.

MERGOLLA. Money.

METROPOLITAN CATHEDRAL. Located in Panama City, the Cathedral was consecrated on April 4, 1796, although construction was begun in 1588. The Cathedral took 108 years and $200,000 to build because fires destroyed the first two attempts. Three of the bells installed in the Cathedral's left tower were brought from Old Panama's Cathedral in 1677.

MIGUEL DE LA BORDA. Cabecera of the Donoso District. Population: 158.

MINIFUNDIO. Very small land holdings. An antonym of latifundio. Generally, very small or tiny land holdings, used by individuals for the purpose of subsistence farming. Varying in size, the plots of land rarely exceed 5 acres in size.

MIRO, Ricardo, 1883-1940. Miró is often considered to be the leading Panamanian Modernist poet. His verse collections, Segundos preludios (1916) and Caminos silenciosos (1929) gave him the honor of being named Panama's national poet. He was also the founder of the review <u>Nuevos ritos</u>.

MITA   see   REPARTIMIENTO.

MOCOCOA.   Vulgarism for sleep or somnolence.

MODERNISMO.   A literary movement which sprang up at
     the beginning of the twentieth century and which was
     a reaction to conformity, naturalism, and literary
     standards of the day.   The earliest figure in the
     movement in Panama was Darío Herrera (1870-1941),
     who was a close friend of Rubén Darío, the leading
     modernista from Nicaragua.   Another Modernist was
     Guillermo Andreve (1879-1940), while the leading
     Panamanian Modernist was Ricardo Miró (1883-1940).

MOLA.   The mola, which is worn as part of the blouse of
     the Cuna Indian women, is a decorative, sewn cloth,
     consisting of pieces of brightly colored fabrics deftly
     sewn together to form complicated geometric or,
     nowadays, anthropomorphic designs in a sort of re-
     verse appliqué.   The bright tones of red, green,
     blue, yellow and black are predominant and are com-
     bined in such a manner as to display the exquisite
     artistic taste of the Cuna woman and her natural
     sense of harmony.   Modern Panamanian women use
     the molas either as part of some outer garment or
     for wall-hangings or other home decoration.

MONROE DOCTRINE.   An oft-misinterpreted piece of U.S.
     foreign policy, the Monroe Doctrine was set forth in
     President Monroe's annual message to Congress on
     December 2, 1823.   There is no one reason for the
     origin of the policy: the background of the doctrine
     may be found in the threat of intervention by the
     Holy Alliance in order to subdue Spain's American
     colonies which were more and more coming into open
     revolt against the mother country.   Further, Russia
     held a most aggressive posture on the northwest
     coast of America and, at the time of the pronounce-
     ment of the Doctrine, distrust of England was rife.
     That nation's Foreign Minister, George Canning, had
     proposed a joint declaration, but national sentiment
     made it impossible for the U.S. President and Con-
     gress to consider such a bilateral statement.
     Monroe, caught in a multilateral squeeze by Euro-
     pean, Asiatic, Latin American, and domestic enti-

ties, thus declared that "...the American continents, by the free and independent condition which they have assumed and maintained, are henceforth not to be considered as subjects for future colonization by any European powers...." and that European intervention in either of the continents could not be viewed "...in any other light than as the manifestation of an unfriendly disposition toward the United States." The Doctrine also made clear that the United States did not intend to take any part "...in the wars of the European powers...." or "...in matters relating to themselves....," i.e., the European powers. Various corollaries and memoranda have been written and voiced since the famous pronouncement of the Doctrine. The last, most important such instance was the Clark Memorandum written in 1928 by J. Reuben Clark, Under-Secretary of State, and made public in March, 1930. In keeping with the Wilson-Hoover-Roosevelt program of peace and good will, the Memorandum declared that the Monroe Doctrine is unilateral; that it does not concern itself purely with inter-American relations, and that the Doctrine is a statement of a case of the U.S. versus Europe, not the U.S. versus Latin America. It goes on to point out that the Doctrine had always been used to protect Latin American nations from European aggression and that the Roosevelt (Theodore) corollary was not a part of the Doctrine in reality, nor did it grow out of the Doctrine. Latin American nations, Panama included, have often misunderstood the intent of the Doctrine, or at worst, totally misinterpreted the Monroe Doctrine as a "hunting license" for the United States.

MONTIJO.   One of eleven distritos in the Province of Veraguas.   Its cabecera is Montijo.

MONTIJO.   Cabecera of the Montijo District.   Population: 768.

MONTUNO.   The male counterpart of the pollera.   The montuno costume, consisting of a shirt (coton) and trousers (chingo), is adorned with picturesque bands of embroidery which are called pintas.   A certain cotton cloth woven on rustic looms which still exist in certain locales is used and the weaving style is tejido de machete or knife weave.   At the present

time, the art has almost disappeared. A specific
hat, special shoes, a woven bag, and certain other
accoutrements are worn to complete the outfit. It is
very easy to over-do the costume and slip from ele-
gance into unartistic flamboyance.

MORACHO. A small reptile of the lizard family.

MORGAN, Henry, 1635-1688. A British pirate and privateer, Sir Henry Morgan is infamous in Panama for
razing Portobelo and marching across the Isthmus to
sack, pillage and burn Panama City (1671). He so
destroyed Panama City that it was moved to a new,
walled site by the Spaniards. The valuables which
he removed from the Isthmus have been calculated in
the millions.

MOSQUETAS. Pendant or hoop earrings with circles of
pearls, which form a part of the pollera outfit.

MUNICIPAL PALACE. Diagonally across from the Metropolitan Cathedral is the Municipal Palace, where the
Declaration of Independence was signed November 3,
1903. Reconstructed in 1909, it is now the seat of
the Municipal Government and the meeting place of
the councilmen for the District of Panamá.

-N-

ÑAFLE. Food, a meal.

NASHVILLE, U.S.S. The U.S.S. Nashville was instrumental in the Panamanian Revolution which brought independence from Colombia. The Nashville, ostensibly
operating under the treaty of 1846 by which the U.S.
had guaranteed the neutrality of the Isthmus and the
maintenance of free tansit there, anchored at Colón.
However, operating under orders from Washington,
the Nashville prevented Colombian forces from crossing the Isthmus to put down the revolt, and four
days later the new government of Panama was formally recognized by the U.S. (November 6, 1903).

NATA. One of six distritos in the Province of Coclé. Its
cabecera is Natá.

NATA.   Cabecera of the Natá District.   Population: 1,530.
Natá is considered one of the oldest towns in the
Western Hemisphere and is one of the few that have
survived in their original sites since colonization by
the Spaniards.   Today, it is a city of contrast, with
one of the oldest churches in the New World juxta-
posed against an ultra-modern Nestlé milk plant.

NATIONAL ANTHEM.   The national anthem, "Alcanzamos
por fin la victoria" (Victory is ours at last), consists of four verses and a chorus.   The words are
by Jerónimo de la Ossa and the music by Santos
Jorge.

NATIONAL FLOWER.   The national flower is the Espíritus
Santos, or Holy Ghost Orchid.

NATIONAL THEATER.   Originally part of a convent used
for musical presentations, it was named the Sarah
Bernhardt Theater in 1894, in honor of the famous
French artist who came to its inauguration.   It was
demolished shortly after the Independence.   Recon-
struction was begun February 15, 1906, and completed two years later.   Its interior is decorated
with works painted in Paris by Roberto Lewis, one
of Panama's outstanding artists.

NATIVISM.   A literary movement which dominated Panamanian literature in the 1920's.   The traditional way of
life was glorified by its adherents.   The leading figures in Panama were Santiago Anguizola (1898-),
Moisés Castillo (1899-), and Ana Isabel Illueca
(1903-).   They may be said to be the literary opponents of the Panama Canal and what that waterway
brought to, or took from, the Panamanian way of
life.

ÑAUPA or ÑA UPA.   In the expression "tiempos de Ña
Upa," it means "long ago" or something very old.

NEW GRANADA.   Upon the dissolution of Gran Colombia in
1830, a new political entity known as New Granada
was formed.   While Venezuela and Ecuador were no
longer included, the new country was huge, far-flung,
and highly disunified, at least geographically.
Panama, which was almost a wild province, was not
initially included in New Granada, owing to its

inaccessibility and relative lasck of importance as an economic factor in the nation.   However, in 1832, Panama became a part of the new nation and was nominally ruled from Bogotá until 1840 when a revolution led to the withdrawal of Panama from New Granada and saw the formation of the Free State of the Isthmus.

NEWSPAPERS.   The following are the major newspapers of the nation.   No reliable circulation figures could be found or obtained.   Panama City: Estrella de Panamá and El Panamá-América, with separate editions in English, are published daily.   The English editions are titled The Star & Herald and The Panama-American, respectively.   The Mundo Gráfico and El Tiempo are published weekly in Panama City. Two dailies are published in David, Ecos del Valle and La Razón.   There is a weekly Atlántico which is published in Colón.

NICUESA, Diego de, 1465-1511.   A rich, pompous man, Nicuesa, along with Alonso de Ojeda, obtained a land grant (called Veragua) in 1508, stretching from Panama northward to Cape Gracias a Dios, to Nicuesa in the west and Ojeda in the east.   In 1510, Nicuesa established a colony called Nombre de Dios near what is now the Caribbean end of the Canal. Hunger and disease reduced the number of his followers from 700 to about 70 men.   Ojeda's expedition (which led to his death) fared still worse, and when Nicuesa attempted to impose his will over the survivors of the Ojeda group and claim all of the gold and pearls found in the Darién, all of the colonists rebelled and put him to sea in a worm-riddled boat which was never seen again.

NIÑO, Pedro Alonso.   In 1522-23, Niño, under authority independent of Pedrarias, led a combined land-sea expedition from the Isthmus, and sailed to Fonseca Bay to the north of Nicaragua.   Earlier, he had been among the most illustrious of the early Spanish mariners who coasted along the northern shores of South America (1499-1500).

NOMBRE DE DIOS.   A colony founded by Nicuesa in 1510 on the Caribbean coast of Panama, east of Portobelo. It was the principal port on the Caribbean side of the Isthmus until the end of the 16th Century, at which time Portobelo surged to the fore. Today the town exists as a ragged fishing village with no importance attached to it.

ÑOÑOCO. Fermented cane juice in the region of Herrera. Corn liquor with small, sun-dried corn balls added to it in the region of Veraguas.

NUEVO CHAGRES. Cabecera of the Chagres District. Population: 234.

NUÑEZ DE BALBOA, Vasco see BALBOA.

-O-

OBALDIA, José Domingo de, 1845-1910. Obaldía, a Conservative, was elected president in 1908. Following party strife in 1908 when a coalition of liberals and conservatives opposed President Amador's efforts to place Ricardo Arias in office as his successor, the U.S., at the request of both the Liberals and Conservatives, appointed a commission to hear electoral complaints. However, Arias withdrew his candidacy and Obaldía was consequently inaugurated. With his death on March 1, 1910, Carlos Antonio Mendoza became temporary executive.

OCU. One of seven distritos in the Province of Herrera. Its cabecera is Ocú.

OCU. Cabecera of the Ocú District, Ocú has a population of 1,121. This town is the home of the montuno, a people who wear the national costume of the same name. Especially interesting are the yards of handmade lace, the homespun fringed suits of the men and the brightly colored full skirts of the women. The town's location is 27 miles west of Chitré.

OJEDA, Alonso de. In concert with Diego de Nicuesa, he obtained, in 1508, a land grant on the Pearl (east) Coast of the Isthmus, running from Cape de la Vela to the Gulf of Urabá. The area was dubbed Urabá. In 1509 he founded the town of San Sebastián which soon foundered and was later moved to a new site by Balboa and given the name of Santa María la Antigua del Darién. Ojeda, attempting to recoup his advan-

tage following terrible pestilence, death and travail,
returned to Hispaniola following a serious wound.
But, unsuccessful in obtaining further support, his
spirit broke, he became a monk and died soon after,
a ghost of his former, flamboyant self.

OLA.   One of six distritos in the Province of Coclé.   Its
cabecera is Olá.

OLA.   Cabecera of the Olá District.   Population: 124.

OSPINA, Gen. Pedro Nel.   President of Colombia as a result of Conservative Party's control of the voting re-
sults.   Ospina was sure enough of his political and
popular support to accept an offer of $25 million by
the U.S. for reparations for loss of Panama.   While
Colombia received no formal apology for the Panamanian Affair, the acceptance of the money by Ospina
laid the groundwork for an excellent financial situation in the country and paved the way for an era
called the "Golden 20's" in Colombia.

OTO.   A short, large-leafed plant whose edible purple roots
are much used in Panamanian cooking.

OTOE   see   OTO.

OXENHAM, John.   An English privateer of the 16th Century
who trying to emulate Sir Francis Drake, attempted
a raid on Panama, was captured by the Spaniards
and executed by the Inquisition in Lima as a heretic.

OYAMA.   An edible gourd.

-P-

PACO.   Policeman.   Cop.

PAIPA.   A metal tube.   From the English, pipe.

PAJARO.   An effeminate man.

PALACIO DE LAS GARZAS, El   see   PRESIDENTIAL
PALACE.

PALACIO MUNICIPAL   see   MUNICIPAL PALACE.

PALENQUE. Cabecera of the Santa Isabel District. Population: 337.

PANAMA (The Republic). The origin of the country's name is confused in etymology. The word panamá came from one of three sources, all indigenous in origin: the word means either "abundance of fish, " or "abundance of butterflies" or is taken from the name of a tree of the same name. The area of the nation is 29, 761 square miles (77, 082 square kilometers), including the Canal Zone which, is 553 square miles in area (1, 432 square kilometers). Capital: Panama City. Official language: Spanish. National flower: Holy Ghost Orchid. Population: 1, 417, 100 (official estimate, 1969) exclusive of the Canal Zone, which in the 1960 Census had a population of 44, 122. Unit of Currency: Balboa (on a par with the U. S. dollar). National Anthem: El Himno Nacional de Panamá. Panama was "discovered" by Columbus in 1498-1500 and named Veraguas. It was not until 1513, when Balboa "discoverd" the Pacific Ocean, that the area assumed any real importance. Panama City was established on the Pacific coast in 1519 and was connected to the Caribbean coast by road and river. Nombre de Dios and Portobelo soon assumed leadership roles as commercial cities maintained by the Spaniards, and Panama became the base for expiditions to Peru and the remainder of Central America. As is true with many parts of the Spanish colonial empire, Panama achieved her independence from Spain in 1821 and joined the Confederation of Gran Colombia. After various political ups and downs Panama finally proclaimed its own independence in 1903 following Colombia's rejection of a treaty which would have enabled the United States to build the trans-Isthmus canal. Leagued with the U. S. , Panama made her break cleanly and permanently from Colombia. In World War II, after a short flirtation with far-right elements, Panama declared war on the Axis powers. A postwar period of political instability shook the nation, with rapid changing governments the rule. This period tended to come to an end in 1952 with the election of José Antonio Remón to the Presidency. Remón, a former commandant of the National Guard, was assassinated in 1955 and another political crisis reigned until 1956. Regular presidential elections were held in that year and every four

years since. On October 11, 1968, President
Arnulfo Arias, who had been inaugurated on October
1, was overthrown by the National Guard and a new
Government, headed by a Provisional Junta, with
Colonel José M. Pinilla as its President, was established. The Junta has announced that new elections
will be held in 1970.

PANAMA. One of the nine provinces of Panama, located in
the south-central part of the nation. Bordered by
the Gulf of Panama on the south; by the Province of
Coclé on the west; by the Province of Colón and the
Comarca of San Blas on the north; by the Province
of Darién on the east. Panama is divided into two
sections by the Panama Canal. It has an area of
4,360 sq. mi. and its capital is the city of Panama.
The ten distritos and their respective cabeceras are:
Panama, Panama; Arraiján, Arraiján; Balboa, San
Miguel; Capira, Capira; Chame, Chame; Chepo,
Chepo; Chimán, Chimán; La Chorrera, La Chorrera;
San Carlos, San Carlos; Taboga, Taboga. Total
population of the province, official estimate of 1969,
is 542,200. Aside from some agriculture and livestock raising, this province is the major industrial
producer of the nation and has a few embryonic
shrimp-freezing plants in operation. It draws a major portion of its income from tourism and, of
course, is supported to a great extent by the Canal.

PANAMA. One of ten distritos in the Province of Panama.
Its cabecera is Panama.

PANAMA. A rather large tree, heavy trunk, with coarse,
lobular leaves. The nation may take its name from
this tree.

PANAMA CANAL. The existing canal was begun in 1880 by
the French, but disease and financial problems defeated them. In 1903, following the successful revolt from Colombia, Panama and the United States
signed a treaty in which the U.S. guaranteed
Panama's independence and paid her $10 million.
On May 4, 1904, the U.S. purchased the French
Canal Company rights and properties for $40 million
and began construction. The huge project was completed in 10 years at a cost approximating $380
million. The S. S. Ancón made the first official

ocean-to-ocean transit on August 15, 1914. In the
fiscal year 1967, there were 14,070 transits, of
which 13,385 were oceangoing vessels of more than
300 Panama Canal net tons. The total of ships carried 92,997,958 long tons of cargo and paid
$82,296,638 in tolls and toll credits. The pre-World
War II traffic peak was 7,479 vessels in 1939.
Transits in fiscal year 1967 set the all-time record.
The largest toll to the Canal was $31,740.30 paid
by the Liberian flag bulk carrier Mythic, a 39,617
gross ton ship, for transit November 10, 1967.
Highest passenger ship toll was $23,603.40 paid by
the British flag liner Canberra on her first transit
June 11, 1962. Smallest toll was 45 cents paid by
Albert H. Oshiver for swimming between Gatun Locks
and Gamboa in December 1962. The longest passenger vessel to transit the Canal was the German flag
Bremen on February 15, 1939. She was 51,731
gross-ton vessel with an overall length of 898.7 feet.
The widest beamed commercial ships to transit are
the oil-ore carriers, San Juan Pioneer and San Juan
Prospector, both 106.4 feet. Record cargo carried
through the Canal up to February 28, 1968, was a-
board the bulk carrier Mythic which had a load of
coal weighing 57,789 tons. Deepest draft authorized
through the Canal is 40 feet. Tolls are levied on a
net tonnage basis, Panama Canal measurement. They
amount to 90 cents a ton for laden ships and 72 cents
unladen. A ship which would otherwise have to sail
around "The Horn" can easily save 10 times the a-
mount of her toll by using the Canal. The average
toll is $6,315. Of the gross investment of $1,600
million in the Canal enterprise over the years, the
U.S. has recovered $1,100 million. The Canal ope-
ration is self-sustaining. It covers the cost of its
operations, pays the U.S. Treasury interest on the
investment, and is financing the Canal's current $90
million improvement program. Vital statistics of
the Canal are: Average time of ship in Canal waters: 14-16 hours. Average time of transit: 8
hours. Length of Canal: 50.76 statue miles.
Length of sea-level sections: 15.02 statute miles.
Width of channel in sea-level sections: 500 feet.
Width in Gatun Lake section: 500-1,000 feet. Width
of lock chambers: 110 feet. Length (usuable) of
lock chambers: 1,000 feet. Height of walls: Approx. 50 to 81 feet. Width of center walls: 60

feet. Number of lock gates: 46, with 92 leaves.
Height of gates: 47 to 82 feet. Thickness of gates:
7 feet. Weight per leaf: 390 to 730 tons. Concrete
used in locks: 4, 500, 000 cubic yards. Total aggre-
gate excavation: Approx. 400, 468, 850 cubic yards
(of which 29, 908, 000 was excavated by the French).
This quantity is equivalent to that in a cube 2, 132
feet on each side, and is 119 times the size of the
Great Pyramid of Giza, or equivalent to the material
which would come from a hole 16. 2 feet square driv-
en completely through the Earth.

PANAMA CANAL TREATY   see   HAY-BUNAU-VARILLA
TREATY.

PANAMA CANAL ZONE.   The Hay-Bunau-Varilla Treaty of
1903 established the Canal Zone in a strip of land
five miles wide on either side of the site of the then
future canal.   The land was granted to the United
States in perpetuity upon payment of $10 million and
an annuity of $250, 000 initially (which has grown to
in excess of $2 million today).   Actual rental pay-
ments are $1, 930, 000, with other considerations
raising the grand total.   The administration, or government, of the Canal Zone is carried out by the
Panama Canal Company, a self-sustaining, corporate
entity of the U. S. Department of Defense.   The President of the United States serves as governor of the
Zone.   The administrative capital of the Zone is
Balboa Heights, on the Pacific Coast near Panama
City and, with some 14, 000 residents, is the largest
U. S. -controlled city within the Zone.   Only employees
of the Panama Canal may live within the Zone, and
the majority of the "Zoniana" are citizens of Panama.
The Zone is divided into two administrative districts,
Balboa in the south with a population of 30, 623 and
Cristobal in the north with 11, 499 residents.   Other
towns within the Zone and under U. S. control are:
Rainbow City (3, 688); Gamboa (3, 489); Balboa (3, 139),
capital of the Balboa District; Paraíso (3, 113); and
Cristobal (817), capital of the Cristobal District.
For discussion of the Canal,   see   PANAMA CANAL
and related topics.

PANAMA CITY.   Panama was founded by Pedrarias on
August 15, 1519 and was the first lasting Spanish settlement on the Pacific Coast.   He moved the seat of

government there from Santa María la Antigua del
Darién. When the original city was destroyed by
Henry Morgan in 1671, a small peninsula some five
miles away was chosen as the site for the new City
of Panama, which was to be later founded officially
on January 21, 1673. The dedication of the city was
made by Fernandez de Córdoba, then Governor of the
area. Alfonso Mercado de Villacorta was appointed
Governor in 1679 following the death of de Córdoba
and brought with him instructions to build a wall a-
round the new city as a defense measure against future pirate raids. De Villacorta died two years later and subsequent governors finished the job at a
total cost of eleven million Spanish pesos. Part of
the wall was demolished in 1856 to make room for
the expansion of the city. Ruins of the wall still
stand near Herrera Plaza. Today, the City is still
the Capital of the Republic and its leading city. It
is a unique blend of old Spain, modern progress, and
the bizarre atmosphere of the Orient. In addition to
being the political cultural center of the nation, it is
also the leading commercial center. The current
population is listed as 542,000 (official estimate,
1969). Located at Latitude N8° 57', and with an al-
titude of 40' above sea-level, it boasts a year-round
average temperature of 79 degrees and a total annual
rainfall of approximately 70 inches. In addition to
being the National Capital, Panama City is the Capital of the Province of Panama and is the cabecera of
the Panama District.

PANAMA CONFERENCE (1826). A Conference called by
Bolívar with the intent of banding together the various
nations of the Western Hemisphere in order to protect against external attack, especially from European
nations. The Conference was a fiasco, since many
nations did not send representatives; several never
arrived for one reason or other; and virtually noth-
ing was accomplished even after the meeting was
held, for national jealousies made any confederation
impossible.

PANAMA LA VIEJA. Old Panama was founded by Pedro
Arias de Avila (Pedrarias) on August 15, 1519, and
soon became known as a "place of marvelous splendor" with some 7,000 homes, many convents and
churches, a cathedral with a four-storied tower, and

many outstanding public buildings.   At the height of
its importance, it outclassed even Lima, Perú in
splendor and commercial activity.   Many expeditions
to the north, south, and west were launched from
this important center of civilization and government.
In 1671, the infamous English buccaneer Henry
Morgan robbed, sacked and burned the city.   The
date of its death is January 28, 1671.   Today, the
Panamanian Government has declared the site to be
a National Park and is gradually restoring the city
to the extent possible and preserving the remainder
for posterity.

PANAMA RAILROAD.   During the first three years following
the discovery of gold in California, thousands crossed
the Isthmus and, owing to the increasing difficulty in
transporting the multitudes, the owners of ferry
boats organized to plan the construction of a railroad
to unite the two oceans.   One of the main organizers
was Aspinwall.   Work was begun in 1850 on the Island of Manzanillo on the Atlantic Coast, where the
City of Colón stands today.   In the construction of
the line, pestilences of all sorts were encountered:
alligators and other reptiles, mosquitoes and sand
flies so numerous that workers had to wear protec-
tive head covering, swamps and, worst of all, malaria and yellow fever.   Irish, Chinese, Jamaican
and Colombian Negroes, consecutively, were used
as the work gangs.   On January 27, 1855, the last
rails were nailed into place and on the following day
the first steam engine crossed the Isthmus.   The
loss of human life during the construction of the
47. 61 mile line has been calculated in excess of
25, 000.

PANDO PEAK.   Second highest point of elevation in the
country; approximately 3, 162 meters (10, 371 feet)
high.   In the Province of Chiriquí.

PANELA.   A block of brown sugar, molded from heated
cane juice.

PAPA.   Used in the expression "estar en la papa, " it
means to be in favor with the government.

PAQUETAZO.   Electoral fraud.

PARADA. A parade or procession.

PARITA. One of seven distritos in the Province of Herrera.
Its cabecera is Parita.

PARITA. Cabecera of the Parita District.   Population:
1, 221.

PATOCA. A poisonous snake.

PATTERSON, Guillermo Jr. Born in Panama City in 1884,
Patterson was a chemist, professor, and lawyer.
He received a Ph. D. from Notre Dame, Indiana in
1912, and a LL. B. from Hamilton College, in 1920.
He held positions at Cornell University, Notre Dame,
and the Instituto Nacional, Escuela de Farmacia and
Escuela Normal from 1912-1925. He was mayor of
Panama City in 1913. He received the Laudy Prize
twice, among other prizes in various scientific and
literary contests. He was the author of Alberto (a
novel published in 1905), A New Method for the De-
termination of Lead (1911), and many others.

PEARL ISLANDS. So named because of the magnificient
pearls once found in the archipelago, the islands
were first sighted by Balboa soon after his discovery
of the Pacific. Raided and plundered by various
Spanish adventurers, the islands were, in the 16th
Century, a popular stop-over for the explorers of
the Panamanian coast.

PEBRE. Food, sustenance.

PEDASI. One of seven distritos in the Province of Los
Santos. Its cabecera is Pedasí.

PEDASI. Cabecera of the Pedasí District.   Population:
854.

PEDRARIAS (Pedro Arias Dávila), 1442 1531. In 1514,
Pedrarias arrived as the new governor of Darién,
bringing with him the Requerimiento, a document of
1513, which was to be read to all natives before the
Spanish could make war on them or establish suzerainty. Pedrarias and Balboa came into conflict and,
despite the fact that Balboa had become his son-in-
law (by proxy), Pedrarias had him beheaded in 1519.

In 1519 Pedrarias also saw to the founding of Panama
City. Ever-ambitious, in 1522 he sent forces to
Guatemala and Honduras to contest the authority and
control of Cortés' forces in these areas. In 1527 he
was removed by the Crown as Governor of Panama,
but continued as Governor of Nicaragua. The ill will
which he engendered among both the Spanish and the
Indians was formidable and it took the power and
mystique of a Father Las Casas to sway the Indians
to Christianity several years after Pedrarias' death.
Ambivalence surrounds the accomplishments of this
famous or infamous personage of Panama's history.

PEGA-PEGA. An herbaceous plant which grows among
briars and brambles and whose seeds stick tenacious-
ly to the clothing or skin.

PEINILLA. Comb. Also, among the country folk, a long
thin, straight, and very sharp machete.

PELONA. Death.

PENONOME. One of six distritos in the Province of Coclé.
Its cabecera is Penonomé.

PENONOME. Capital of the Province of Coclé and cabecera
of the Penonomé District, the town has a population
of 4,266 (1960). Today the town is an important
collection and pick-up point for agricultural products
of the central provinces, as well as a stopover for
truckers. Penonomé dates back to the conquistadores, and has been the site of many interesting
finds of pre-Columbian artifacts.

PERRENCAZO. A drink or "shot" of liquor.

PESE. Cabecera of the Pesé District. Population: 1,323.

PESE. One of seven distritos in the Province of Herrera.
Its cabecera is Pesé.

PICA PIEDRA. A yellowish, nocturnal bird, with a rather
disagreeable song.

PICA-RIO. A small shore or river bird of the fishing
Martin family.

PICACHO PEAK. Seventh highest point of elevation in the
country; approximately 2,000 meters (6,560 feet)
high. In the Province of Chiriquí.

PICAFLOR. A woman-chaser, a playboy.

PICOGORDO. A small song bird whose plumage changes
colors as it matures.

PINDIN. A dance of the central provinces of Panama.

PINILLA, Mosé M. President of the Provisional Junta of
Government, 1968- .

PINILLA FABREGA, Col. José María. When the Guardia
Nacional deposed President Arnulfo Arias on October
12, 1968, a military junta, headed by Col. José
María Pinilla Fábrega took over the government
while Arias fled first to the Canal Zone and later to
the U.S. Colonel Pinilla is a career officer in the
Guardia and tends to be associated with the wealthy
leadership of the nation, particularly the larger land
owners and business interests.

PINO RAPHAEL, Antonio. Born in David, Panamá in 1908.
He was named consul general, San Francisco, California (1936-37), general administrator of customs
(1940-41), secretary of the treasury department
(1941-43), and director of the post office and tele-
communications (1943- .)

PINOGANA. One of two distritos in the Province of Darién.
Its cabecera is El Real.

PISBA, PIBA, or PIFA. A member of the palm family.
Also bears the name of pisbae, pixbae, and pejibaye.

PIZARRO, Francisco, 1474-1541. This shrewd, but illite-
rate, Spanish adventurer started his conquest expedition of the Incas from Panama in 1531 after two earlier false starts in 1524 and 1526 by him and his
partners, Almagro and Luque. It was only after special concessions and backing from the Crown and following successful efforts to enlist additional help in
Spain (including his brothers, Hernando, Gonzalo, and
Juan) that Pizarro was able to begin the phenomenal
conquest for which he is so well known.

PLEQUE-PLEQUE. A heated discussion or argument. A scandal or fight.

POCRI. Cabecera of the Pocrí District. Population: 570.

POCRI. One of seven distritos in the Province of Los Santos. Its cabecera is Pocrí.

POLITICAL PARTIES. Until recent days, there were ten national and eighteen municipally oriented political parties in operation in Panama. On March 3, 1969, by Cabinet Decree No. 58, all political parties were abolished. Therefore, as of this writing, there are no political parties legally in existence in the nation. The ten national parties were: Acción Democrática (P. A. D.); Coalición Patriótica Nacional (C. P. N.); Demócrata Cristiano (P. D. C.); Laborista Cristiano (P. L. C.); Liberal Nacional (P. L. N.); Movimiento de Liberación Nacional (M. L. N.); Panameñista (P. P.); Progresista (P. P.); Republicano (P. R.); and Tercer Partido Nacionalista (T. P. N.). The eighteen municipal parties and their locations were: Partido Municipal Abuerma (P. M. A.), Bocas del Toro; Partido Municipal Integración Laboral (P. M. I. L.), Bocas del Toro; Partido Bloque Aguadulceño (P. B. A.), Aguadulce; Partido Social Obrero Luchador (P. S. O. L.), Antón; Partido Acción Progresista (P. A. P.), Penonomé; Partido Acción Purificadora Colonense (P. A. P. C.), Colón; Partido Popular Colonense (P. P. C.), Colón; Partido Juventud Democrática Colonense (P. J. D. C.), Colón; Partido Cívico del Barú (P. C. B.), Barú, Chiriquí; Partido Movimiento Revolucionario Municipal de Chitré (P. M. R. M. C.), Chitré; Partido Municipal 28 de Noviembre (P. M. V. N.), Las Tablas; Partido Municipal Acción Arraijaneña (P. M. A. A.), Arraiján; Partido Municipal Alianza Campesina Arraijaneña (P. M. A. C. A.), Arraiján; Partido Municipal Movimiento de Acción Renovadora Chorrerana Avante (P. M. M. A. R. C. A.), Chorrera; Partido Municipal Unión Chorrerana (P. M. U. C.), Chorrera; Partido Municipal Humildes Unificados (P. M. H. U.), Panama; Partido Municipal Industrial Progresista (P. M. I. P.), Panama; Partido Municipal Renovación Popular Auténtica (P. R. P. A.), Panama.

POLLERA. The pollera is Panama's most authentic "native" feminine attire. This classic garment which was

worn in colonial times is still the pride of many women. It is, in effect, the "National Costume of
Panamá." Basically, the pollera is a two-piece outfit: a blouse or camisa and a skirt or pollerón.
Two elaborate lace-fringed linen petticoats are worn
beneath the skirt. The blouse is a fancy piece of
handwork with two ruffles, one waist-length and a
shorter, overlapping sleeve. Both are elaborately
decorated with hand-sewn, cross-stitched and shad-
owed designs with one or two rows of lace insertion
of the same color as the design. The ankle-length
pollerón is bell-shaped, gradually tapering outward
from the waist to the lace-trimmed hemline several
yards in width. All cross-stitched, it has an upper
and lower section, divided by a row of 2 1/2-inch
lace insert. Two strips of ribbon, of the same col-
or as the pom-poms used, hang in front from the
waistline to about halfway down the upper section of
the skirt. Matching heelless slippers and specific
jewelry, normally gold handmade items, are worn
with the outfit. There are other less elegant models,
such as the montuna, the campesina and the Ata-
layera. Also, a native dance.

PORO-PORO. A tree which varies between 5 and 12 meters in height; alternate 5-lobed leaves. The wood
is soft and spongy.

PORRAS, Dr. Belisario. Dr. Porras, who came to the
Presidency at the head of the Liberals in the dubious
elections of 1912, was to dominate Panamanian poli-
tics for some twelve years. He declined U.S. super-
vision of the 1916 elections, which caused the Conservatives again to withdraw from the contest.
Ramón Valdés, his follower, then took office but
died two years later. Porras again assumed the
presidency, but only after a violent controversy during which U.S. troops policed Panama City and Colón.
The U.S. again politically intervened in 1918 in order
to bring order to what it considered total chaos in
controlling the nation's police force and the sale of
drugs and other undesirable commodities among the
U.S. troops stationed in the Zone. Porras resigned
shortly before the election of 1920 in order once
more to be eligible--and was reelected. Perhaps the
chief event of this last reign was a short-lived war,
or boundary dispute, with the Republic of Costa Rica.

Costa Rica lost, but under prodding from the U.S.,
Panama observed the right of Costa Rica to occupy
the Coto region which had been awarded to the latter nation by the President of France in 1900 and,
in essence, re-awarded by Chief Justice White of
the U.S. Supreme Court in 1914. Rodolfo Chiari,
a political associate of Dr. Porras, became president in 1924.

PORRAS PLAZA. Known as Cervantes Plaza from 1916
until 1948, it was renamed Porras Plaza to honor
Dr. Belisario Porras, President of the Republic for
ten consecutive years.

PORTOBELO. One of five distritos in the Province of
Colón. Its cabecera is Portobelo.

PORTOBELO. The cabecera of the Portobelo District, the
town today has shrunk to 511 people. With a history
dating back to Columbus' fourth voyage, when he
purportedly sailed into its great harbor in 1502 and
exclaimed "Porto bello!" (Beautiful port!), the city
was officially founded in 1597. It flourished as the
greatest trading center in the world during the 17th
and 18th centuries, with up to 1500 craft at anchor
at one time in the harbor. Today, Portobelo is
virtually a ghost town, stirring to life only during
the Feast of the Black Christ on October 21 of each
year. The celebration is in honor of a rather mi-
raculous statue made of cocobolo wood which is too
heavy to float. Legend has it that when a ship tried
to move the statue, which was being transhipped
from Spain to Colombia, the ship could not leave
Portobelo and, when the crew threw the statue over-
board, it miraculously floated to shore where the
townspeople rescued it and have guarded it ever
since. The ruins of the three major forts of San
Gerónimo, Santiago la Gloria, and San Fernando are
found here. Henry Morgan sacked the town and, although it was rebuilt, it never again reached its former state of glory or commercial importance.

PRESIDENTIAL PALACE. Also called El Palacio de las
Garzas (The Palace of the Herons) because of the
long-necked birds hovering around the fountain in the
main entrance patio. First erected in 1673, it was
completely reconstructed in 1921 by President

Belisario Porras to serve as the Presidential Mansion. Its main feature is the Yellow Room, with murals by Roberto Lewis and portraits of the country's rulers.

PRESIDENTS OF PANAMA. (A complete list of all rulers from the first constitutional president in 1904 to date, including acting presidents. Dates indicate terms of office.) see also SPANISH GOVERNORS and GOVERNORS OF THE GRANADINE AND COLOMBIAN ERA.

Arango, José Augstín, 1903-1904.

Boyd, Federico, 1903-1904, 1910.

Arias, Tomás, 1903-1904.

Espinosa Batista, Manuel (Provisional Government Junta), 1903-1904.

Amador Guerrero, Manuel (First Constitutional President), 1904-1907, 1907-1908.

de Obaldía, José Domingo, 1907, 1908-1910.

Mendoza, Carlos Antonio, 1910.

Arosemena, Pablo, 1910-1912, 1912.

Chiari, Rodolfo (interim), 1912, 1923, 1924-1928, 1928.

Porras, Belisario, 1912-1916, 1918-1920, 1920-1923, 1923-1924.

Valdés, Ramón Maximiliano, 1916-1918.

Urriola, Ciro Luis, 1918.

Díaz, Pedro Antonio, 1918.

Tisdel Lefevre, Ernesto, 1920.

Duque, Tomás Gabriel (transitory), 1928.

Arosemena, Florencio Harmodio, 1928-1931.

Arias Madrid, Harmodio, 1931, 1932-1933, 1933-1936.

Alfaro, Ricardo Joaquín, 1931-1932.

Díaz Arosemena, Domingo, 1933, 1948-1949.

Arosemena, Juan Demóstenes, 1936-1939.

Fernández Jaén, Ezequiel, 1939.

Boyd, Augusto Samuel, 1939-1940.

Arias Madrid, Arnulfo, 1940-1941, 1949-1951.

Pezet, José, 1941.

Jaén Guardia, Ernesto, 1941.

de la Guardia, Ricardo Adolfo, 1941-1945.

Jiménez, Enrique Adolfo, 1945-1948.

Chanis Jr., Daniel, 1949, 1949.

Chiari, Roberto Francisco, 1949, 1960-1961, 1961-1962, 1963, 1963-1964.

Arosemena, Alcibíades, 1951-1952.

Remón Cantera, José Antonio, 1952-1953, 1954-1955.
Guizado, José Ramón, 1953.
Arias Espinosa, Ricardo Manuel, 1954, 1955.
de la Guardia, Jr., Ernesto, 1956-1960.
González Ruiz, Sergio, 1961, 1962.
Bazán, José Dominador 1962-1963.
González Ruiz, Bernardino, 1963.
Robles, Marcos Aurelio, 1964-1968.
Arias, Arnulfo, 1968.
Pinilla, José M. 1968- .

PROVINCIA. The provincia, or province, is the largest
    political division within the Republic, the equivalent
    of a state in the United States. There are 9 prov-
    inces and one territory (San Blas) which is normally
    included in the Province of Colón. The provinces
    are: Bocas del Toro; Coclé; Colón; Chiriquí;
    Darién; Herrera; Los Santos; Panama, and Veraguas.

PUERTO ARMUELLES. Cabecera of the Barú District. Pop-
    ulation: 5,734.

PUNTA DEL ESTE CONFERENCE. At a meeting of the
    American foreign ministers held at Punta del Este,
    Uruguay (January, 1962), to consider the "Cuban
    situation," Panama joined five other Latin American
    nations in voting against sanctions against Cuba, but
    resolutions to exclude Cuba from the inter-American
    system and the Inter-American Defense Board, and
    the imposition of an arms embargo were passed.

-Q-

QUINCHA. From Quechua. A wall of quincha, which is a
    barrier of poles crossed by a series of transverse
    cane pieces, covered with a thick clay with straw in
    it to give it consistency.

-R-

RABIBLANCO. A term applied in an ironic sense to people
    of the upper social strata.

RACAMACANO. Said of things that are good, effective, or
    vigorous.

REAL. A silver coin, with a value of ten centésimos of a
Balboa. In older days, a silver coin worth 10 centa-
vos of a peso.

REBOLINCHO. Disturbance, tumult, riot.

RECOPILACION DE LEYES DE INDIES. The collection of
laws and regulations relating to the Spanish colonies,
first published in 1563. Revisions were brought out
in 1596, 1628 and 1681. The Spanish government
published a definitive edition in 1681 which was not
revised until 1805. The Leyes covered all aspects
of colonial life, including the Church, finances, the
Indians and slavery. It contained many humanitarian
regulations, but was so detailed that it could not be
effectively enforced.

REFRITO. A sauce made of onions, red peppers, tomato,
achiote (bixa orellana), or other coloring matter, and
cooked in oil.

REGIDOR. An alderman on the municipal council. In the
early colonial period, the regidor was elected by the
inhabitants of a community, but later the post was
sold by the crown and often became hereditary. The
position became and remains little more than an honorary title.

REMEDIOS. One of twelve distritos in the Province of
Chiriquí. Its cabecera is Remedios.

REMEDIOS. Cabecera of the Remedios District. Population: 1,052.

REMON, Col. José. The elections of 1952 saw Colonel
José Remón emerge victorious. As chief of police,
he was perhaps the most powerful man in the country and, some claim, the most wealthy. He was
quite friendly toward the U.S. and, owing to a lull
in anti-U.S. feeling, things were quiet. Under his
regime, the U.S. agreed to raise the annual rental
for the Canal from $430,000 to $2 million. Many
improvements were made on the Canal under his
leadership. Remón also boosted tourism in the nation and brought about a decided increase in light
and mildly heavy industry. However, a pet project
of his, the resettlement of the idle proletariat on

farmland, was almost a total failure. Remón was
shot dead at a race track in January, 1955. Following a short period of confusion, Ernesto de la
Guardia, backed by extreme nationalists and the
Communist party, was installed as President.

REMON-EISENHOWER TREATY. A "treaty of mutual understanding and cooperation, " this agreement was signed
January 25, 1955. The intent of the agreement,
which was originated by President Remón of Panama,
was to gain further concessions from the United
States relating to the Canal Treaty. Under this treaty a number of important accomplishments were at-
tained including a boost in annual payments and the
return of certain pieces of land.

REPARTIMIENTO. The word means a "distribution. " Much
confusion surrounds this word historically, for it is
used to describe the distribution of Indians among the
Spaniards in encomiendas and is also used in connection with the forced sale of goods to the Indians of
various areas of the New World. The term was initially applied to a system of draft labor authorized
by the Spanish Crown in places where workers were
needed to cultivate fields, handle livestock, or oper-
ate mines. There were also repartimientos for public works. Wages and working conditions were regu-
lated and all but a few Indians in privileged positions,
such as artisans or farmers working their own lands,
were forced to work. The system was often referred
to by the Quechua word, mita.

REQUERIMIENTO. An odd document promulgated by the
Spanish Crown in 1513 which was to be read to all
natives before the Spanish could make war on them
or establish suzerainty. Essentially, it consisted of
a brief history of the Christian world, an explanation
of the Papacy, a statement that the Pope had awarded
part of the world to the Spanish Crown, that they
(the natives) were residing on lands owned by the
Crown and were summoned to pay allegiance to the
Crown and assume the Holy Roman Catholic religion.
Pedrarias carried the requerimiento with him when
he first colonized Panama.

RESBALADERA. A refreshment, i. e. , drink, prepared
from a barley base.

RESCATE. A sanctioned Spanish government system of the
   purchase of slaves from Indian groups. The system
   soon broke down owing to fraud and abuse.

RESIDENCIA. During the Colonial Era, the residencia was
   a public investigation of all officials, including the
   viceroys, upon their relinquishing their office. A
   judge especially appointed for the purpose heard any
   and all complaints and, since all who presented griev-
   ances were held safe from retaliation, scandals were
   often produced. Even viceroys could, theoretically,
   be made to make reparation for any injustices com-
   mitted during their tenure in office. The principal
   effect of the system was to discourage any real ini-
   tiative by political figures, leaving them to carry out
   only the specific duties of their offices for fear of
   having exceeded their authority.

REYES, Gen. Rafael. Colombia's loss of Panama engendered a new political system in that nation. Reyes
   may be said to have gained the Presidency of
   Colombia because of the independence of Panama.
   His "system" endured from 1904 until about 1930 (he
   was actually in office 1904-1909). Under his guid-
   ance, a period of general prosperity came to
   Colombia, and an era of internal peace reigned for
   vears.

RIO DE JESUS. One of eleven distritos in the Province of
   Veraguas. Its cabecera is Río de Jesús.

RIO DE JESUS. Cabecera of the Río de Jesús District.
   Population: 1,020.

ROBALO PEAK. Fifth highest point of elevation in the
   country; approximately 2,175 meters (7,144 feet)
   high. In the Province of Bocas del Toro.

ROMANTICISM. A literary movement which spread from
   Spain to most of Latin America during the last part
   of the nineteenth century. The school is character-
   ized by more individualism and freedom from the
   established forms. Although there were a number
   of poets and prose writers in Panama during this
   period, none may be said to be truly outstanding.

ROOSEVELT, Franklin D., 1882-1945. A general policy of

good will toward the Latin American nations was formalized in the "Good Neighbor Policy" of FDR in 1933. Particularly significant to Panama was the 7th Pan American Conference (Montevideo, December, 1933) during which Secretary of State Cordell Hull pronounced the policy of nonintervention. In pursuance of that policy, a treaty was signed in March, 1936 and ratified in 1939, whereby the U.S. surrendered its right to intervention in the internal affairs of the Republic and also withdrew its guarantee of Panama's independence.

ROOSEVELT, Theodore, 1858-1919. It was under Teddy Roosevelt's rule that the climax of the period of "manifest destiny" in the United States' history was reached. Through a series of events, including the U.S.-Mexican War, the Gadsden Purchase, the Spanish American War, the Platt Amendment on Cuba, and the independence of Panama, the U.S. came to exercise more and more power over her neighbors to the south. Undoubtedly, Panama owes a great deal of her independence from Colombia to Roosevelt, but we still inherit the title of "Dollar Diplomacy" to this day. In fairness, however, it should be noted that during his second term in office, the attitudes of Roosevelt and of the U.S. took a different tack, leading to a period of relative good will, culminating in the Good Neighbor Policy of Franklin D. Roosevelt's administration. Roosevelt presents an anomoly especially for Panamanians and peoples of many other nations. The "Big Stick Policy" will linger long in the mind of the world.

ROZA. Among the farmers, land sown in rice or corn.

RUANA. A square cape with a head-hole in the center. A poncho.

RUCANO. A name given to certain silver coins, e.g., the Balboa, the dollar, the peso.

RUIZ GARRIDO, Ana Isabel. Born in Panama City in 1910, Miss Ruiz Garrido went to Roedean School, Brighton, England and the Royal Academy of Music, London. She taught piano at the Conservatorio Nacional de Música. She received a gold medal from the London Academy of Music.

-S-

SAGUILA.   From Cuna.   Chief of a community of Cuna Indians.

SAHILA   see   SAGUILA.

SAINT JOSEPH'S CHURCH OF THE GOLDEN ALTAR.   Virtually destroyed in Morgan's rape of Old Panama, the church was moved to the present Panama City along with its Golden Altar for which it is so famed.

SAINT-MALO, Alfredo de.   Born in Panama City in 1898. Saint-Malo, an excellent violinist, attended the Instituto Nacional de Panamá and the Conservatoie Nationale de Musique, Paris.   He was the director of the Conservatorio Nacional de Música y Declamación de Panamá beginning in 1941.

SALOMA.   A peculiar falsetto tonal sound emitted with pauses or hesitations, with periods of intensity of sound, interspersed with phrasing or verses.   This "singing" has been used historically by the Panamanian farmer to break the monotony of his solitary labor.   Can be roughly approximated to sea chanteys.

SAN BLAS INDIANS   see   CUNA INDIANS.

SAN BLAS MOUNTAINS   see CORDILLERA DE SAN BLAS.

SAN CARLOS.   One of ten distritos in the Province of Panama.   Its cabecera is San Carlos.

SAN CARLOS.   Cabecera of the San Carlos District.   Population: 438.

SAN FELIX.   One of twelve distritos in the Province of Chiriquí.   Its cabecera is Las Lajas.

SAN FRANCISCO.   One of eleven distritos in the Province of Veraguas.   Its cabecera is San Francisco.

SAN FRANCISCO.   Cabecera of the San Francisco District. Population: 814.

SAN LORENZO.   One of twelve distritos in the Province of Chiriquí.   Its cabecera is Horconcitos.

SAN MIGUEL. Cabecera of the Balboa District. Popula-
    tion: 1,291.

SAN SEBASTIAN. The first town founded (1508) by Alonso
    de Ojeda in Urabá. The settlement, located on the
    east coast of the Gulf of Urabá, was abandoned in
    1509 when de Ojeda founded Santa María la Antigua
    del Darién and moved his headquarters to that city.

SANCOCHO. A typical Panamanian food, prepared with
    breast meat from a chicken, yucca, yam, plantain,
    coriander, and oregano. It is approximately like a
    thick soup or a stew.

SANTA ANA PLAZA. Once the site of the first houses
    built in the new City of Panama, it became a public
    square November 28, 1890. At one side of the
    Plaza is the Santa Ana Church, built in 1764.

SANTA FE. One of eleven distritos in the Province of
    Veraguas. Its cabecera is Santa Fé.

SANTA FE. Cabecera of the Santa Fé District. Population:
    414.

SANTA ISABEL. One of five distritos in the Province of
    Colón. Its cabecera is Palenque.

SANTA MARIA. One of seven distritos in the Province of
    Herrera. Its cabecera is Santa María.

SANTA MARIA. Cabecera of the Santa Maria District.
    Population: 815.

SANTA MARIA DE BELEN. A short-lived town founded by
    Columbus on February 24, 1503 on the Caribbean side
    of the Isthmus. The town represented the first Euro-
    pean attempt at colonization of the mainland of the
    New World.

SANTA MARIA LA ANTIGUA DEL DARIEN. The second
    town founded by Alonso de Ojeda on the west coast
    of the Gulf of Urabá (1509). The town served as the
    seat of government until Pedrarias established
    Panama in 1519.

SANTA MARIA RIVER. Fourth longest river in the country;

127 kilometers (80 miles) long, draining an area of 2,580 square kilometers. In the Provinces of Veraguas, Herrera and Coclé.

SANTIAGO. One of eleven distritos in the Province of Veraguas. Its cabecera is Santiago.

SANTIAGO. Capital of the Province of Veraguas and cabecera of the Santiago District, the town of Santiago had a 1960 population of 8,746. It is best known as a collection and way station for truckers.

SANTIAGO PEAK. Third highest point of elevation in the country; approximately 2,826 meters (9,269 feet) high. In the Province of Chiriqui.

SAPA. A spy or secret observer. Also, a member of the Secret Police.

SERRANIA DEL DARIEN. An 8 to 10-mile wide Caribbean coastal mountain range, generally low (to 3,600 feet) and gently contoured, but rising to over 6,000 feet and becoming rugged near the Colombian border. An easterly extension of the Cordillera de San Blas.

SIERRA DE CHIRIQUI. Western portion of Cordillera de Talamanca.

SIERRA DE VERAGUAS. Eastern portion of Cordillera de Talamanca.

SINAN, Rogelio. Pseudonym. See DOMINGUEZ ALBA, Bernardo.

SOCABON. A rustic, four-stringed guitar, also called a bocona.

SONA. One of eleven distritos in the Province of Veraguas. Its cabecera is Soná.

SONA. Cabecera of the Soná District. Population: 2,037. Soná has experienced a phenomenal growth in the past ten years, owing to its emergence as a collection and shipping center for the agricultural and stock-raising area in which it is located.

SOUTH SEA. Name given by Balboa to the Pacific Ocean.

SPANISH GOVERNORS OF PANAMA. (A complete list of all
    rulers, nominal or actual, of all or parts of Panama
    from the first istant of Spanish political incursion un-
    til independence from Spain was accomplished. Dates
    indicate terms of office.) see also PRESIDENTS OF
    PANAMA and GOVERNORS OF THE GRANADINE AND
    COLOMBIAN ERA.
de Nicuesa, Diego, 1510-1511.
Núñez de Balboa, Vasco, 1511-1514.
Arias Dávila, Pedro (Pedrarias), 1514-1526.
de Sosa, Lope (Named but never served) 1526.
de los Ríos, Pedro, 1526-1529.
de la Gama, Antonio, 1529-1532.
Barrionuevo, Francisco, 1533-1536.
de Andagoya, Pascual, 1535.
Velásquez de Acuña, Pedro, 1536-1539.
Vaca de Castro, Cristóbal (transitory), 1540.
First Magistrates of the Real Audiencia of Panamá:
    Francisco Pérez de Robles, Páez de la Serna, Pedro
    de Villalobos, Alfonso de Montenegro, 1539-1543.
Núñez Vela, Blasco (under extraordinary powers),
    1544.
Ramírez de Quiñones, Pedro, 1543-1545, 1548, 1576-
    1585.
Casaus, Pedro, 1545.
de Herrera, Diego, 1545.
de Bachicao, Hernando, 1545-1546.
de Rivero, Pedro, 1546.
de Hinojosa, Pedro Antonio, 1546.
de la Gasca, Pedro, 1546.
de Alvarez, Alonso, 1546-1548.
de Vallecillo, Juan Barba, 1549-1550.
de Clavijo, Sancho, 1550-1553.
de Contreras, Hernando, 1550.
de Contreras, Pedro, 1550.
de Sosa, Alvaro, 1553-1556.
de Barbosa, Juan, 1556.
Ruiz de Monjarás, Juan, 1557-1559.
de Figuerola, Rafael, 1559-1561.
de Guzmán, Luis, 1561-1563.
Busto de Villegas, Juan (died before occupying office),
    1563.
García de Castro, Lope, 1563-1564.
Barros de San Millán, Manuel, 1565-1566, 1567-1569.
Arias de Herrera y Maldonado, Alonso, 1566.
de Pinedo, Juan, 1566.
Lope de Vera, Diego, 1569-1573.

Loarte, Gabriel, 1573-1578.
López de Cepeda, Juan (interim), 1578.
del Barrio Sepúlveda, Juan, 1585-1587, (interim) 1596.
de Cárdenas, Francisco, 1587-1596.
Sotomayor y Andía, Alonso, 1596-1602.
de Añazco, Hernando (interim), 1602-1604, (proprietorship) 1604-1605.
Valverde de Mercado, Francisco, 1605-1614.
Manso de Contreras, Francisco, 1614-1616.
Fernández de Velasco, Diego, 1616-1619.
de la Cruz Rivadeneira, Juan, 1619-1621.
Chávez, Roque, 1621.
Vivero y Velasco, Rodrigo, 1621-1627.
de Colmenares Andrade, Juan (named but never served), 1627.
Brienda y Cárdenas, Francisco (named but declined office), 1627.
de Quiñones Osorio, Alvaro, 1627-1632.
Hurtado de Corcuera, Sebastián, 1632-1634.
Henríquez de Sotomayor, Enrique, 1634-1638.
de León, Andrés Garabito (interim), 1638.
de la Motta Sarmiento, Iñigo, 1638-1642.
de la Vega y Bazán, Juan, 1643-1646.
Fernández de Córdoba y Croalla, Juan, 1646-1649.
Barba Vallecillo, Juan, 1649-1650.
de Bitrián Navarra y Biamonte (interim), 1650-1651.
de Orosco, Diego (interim), 1651.
Guzmán de Toledo, Francisco (interim), 1651.
Hurtado de Corcuera, Sebastián (named, but declined office), 1651.
Herrera y Henríquez, Francisco (named, but declined office), 1651.
Carrilla de Guzmán, Pedro, 1652-1657.
Ibáñez de la Riva Aguero, Fernando, 1658-1663.
Figueroa, Pablo, 1663-1665.
Pérez de Guzmán y Gonzaga, Juan, 1665-1667, (reinstalled), 1669-1671.
de Bracamonte Jr., Agustín, 1667-1669.
de Ibarra, Diego (interim), 1669, (declined office) 1671.
Losada Quiñones, Luis (Real Audiencia Magistrate), 1671.
Martínez de Amileta, Andrés (Real Audiencia Magistrate), 1671.
de Marichelar, Francisco Miguel (Ecc. Judge Instructor), 1671.

Fernández de Córdoba y Mendoza, Antonio, 1671-1673.
de León, Antonio (Bishop), 1673-1675.
de Marichelar, Francisco Miguel, 1675-1676.
Mercado de Villacorta, Alonso, 1676-1681.
Fernández de Piedrahita, Lucas, 1681-1682.
Alzamora, José, 1682.
Ponte de Liorena, Pedro (Count of Palmar), 1682-1690.
de Guzmán Dávalos, Pedro José (Marquis de Mina), 1690-1695.
Ladrón de Guevara, Diego, 1695-1696.
Henríquez de Guzmán, Pedro Luis (Count of Canillas), 1696-1699, 1699-1702.
de la Rocha y Carranza, José Antonio (Marquis of Villarrocha), 1699, 1706-1708, 1711.
D'Avila Bravo de Laguna, Fernando, 1702-1706.
Vicentelo Toledo y Luca, Juan Eustaquio (Marquis of Brenes), 1706-1708.
Haro de Monterroso, Fernando, 1708.
de Urueta e Irusta, Juan Bautista (Real Audiencia), 1708-1710.
de la Rañeta y Vera, Juan, 1710-1711.
Hurtado de Amézaga, José, 1711-1718.
Llamas y Rivas, Juan José (Bishop of Panamá), 1718.
Vadillo, Jerónimo, 1718-1723.
Pérez Buelta, Gaspar, 1723-1724.
Alzamora y Ursino, José (interim), 1724.
de Aldrete, Manuel, 1724-1730.
Vivero y Velasco, Juan José Andía (Marquis of Villa Hermosa), 1730-1735.
Martínez de la Vega, Dionisio, 1735-1743.
de Alcedo Ugarte y 'Herrera, Dionisio, 1743-1749.
de Montiano, Manuel, 1749-1758.
Guil y Gonzaga, Antonio, 1758-1761.
Roan, José (interim), 1762.
de Arana y Górnica, José, 1762-1764.
Blasco de Orosco, José, 1764-1767.
Cabrejo, Joaquín, 1767.
de Agreda, Manuel, 1767-1768.
de Castro, Nicolás, 1768-1769, 1772.
de Olaciregui, Vicente, 1770-1772.
Quijano, Nicolás, 1773-1774.
Navas, Francisco, 1774.
Carbonel y Pinto, Pedro, 1774-1779.
de Carvajal, Ramón, 1779-1785.

Dómas y Valle, José, 1786-1793.
Narváea y la Torre, Antonio, 1793-1803.
de Marcos Urbina, Juan, 1803-1805.
de la Mata, Juan Antonio, 1805-1812.
Pérez, Benito (Viceroy of New Granada), 1812-1813.
Somodeville, Víctor Salcedo, 1813.
Meynar, Carlos, 1813-1815.
de Ayala, Francisco, 1815-1816.
Alvarez, José, 1816.
de Iturralde, Juan Domingo, 1816-1817.
de Hore, Alejandro, 1817-1820.
Ruiz de Porras, Pedro, 1820.
Aguilar, Francisco, 1820.
de Sámano y Urribarry, Juan (Viceroy of New
    Granada), 1820-1821.
Cires, Tomás, 1821.
de la Cruz Murgeón, Juan, 1821.
de Fábrega, José, 1821-1822.

SPOONER ACT. An Act of the United States Congress in
    1902, authorizing the President (Roosevelt) to under-
    take the work of constructing a trans-Isthmian Canal
    through Panama.

STATE OF THE ISTHMUS. In 1840, Tomás Herrera led a
    revolution which was successful in withdrawing
    Panama from New Granada. Colonel Herrera was
    named head of the new state, November, 1840, and
    Costa Rica recognized the new nation. Herrera sent
    an envoy to the United States to establish diplomatic
    relations, but an accord was never reached. During
    the 13 months of its existence, the State of the
    Isthmus developed an embryonic constitution and saw
    economic and diplomatic relations begin to develop.
    Soon, however, New Granada turned its attention to
    the break-away state and, following protracted bar-
    gaining, Panama was rejoined to New Granada on
    December 31, 1841.

SUSTO, Juan Antonio. An archivist and historian, Susto
    was born in Panama City in 1896. He studied at the
    Instituto Nacional from 1912-1913, the Colegio La
    Salle, 1917, did special studies in archives of Costa
    Rica, 1918, and of Sevilla, Spain, 1923-1930. He
    was a member of the ministry of interior and justice
    in 1918. He received first prizes in contests spon-
    sored by the Instituto Nacional in 1918 and 1920. He

was named the "Adopted Son" of the city of Sevilla
in 1930, and was the author of many works including
Panamá en el Archivo General de Indias, (1917), Don
Miguiel José de Ayala (1930), etc.

-T-

TABANCO. A rustic stove or fireplace used for cooking in
the field.

TABOGA. One of ten distritos in the Province of Panama.
Its cabecera is Taboga.

TABOGA. Cabecera of the Taboga District. Population:
856. Taboga, which is an island, is located 11
miles south of Balboa on the Pacific side of the
isthmus and is a favored summer resort. Remains
of Spanish fortifications are still visible on parts of
the island. Tourism is the main concern of Toboga
today.

TACARCUNA PEAK. Fourth highest point of elevation in
the country; approximately 2,280 meters (7,478 feet)
high. In the Province of Darién.

TAFT AGREEMENT. In 1904 President Roosevelt opened
the Canal Zone to commerce and established post
offices and customs houses there. The Panamanian
Government strenuously objected, however, maintain-
ing that the Canal Treaty did not give the U.S. the
right to take measures which threatened Panama's
trade or crippled her finances. When Secretary of
War Taft visited the Isthmus in the autumn of 1904,
the Taft Agreement was arranged. By this agreement, imports into the Zone were limited, in general,
to goods for the use of the U.S. and its employees
or for sale to vessels passing through the Canal.
The general public was not to be permitted to trade
at the commissaries which the U.S. authorities established. In principle, the agreement has worked.
In practice, the situation which gave rise to it per-
sists to this day.

TAJONA. A whip, the word being used in the Los Santos
area. In Veraguas and Chiriquí, the word mulero
is used, while in the remainder of the provinces the

word is garrotillo.

TALAMANCA MOUNTAIN RANGE see CORDILLERA DE TALAMANCA.

TALINGO. A bird with black plumage, a long tail and thick beak, which feeds on ticks and other parasites infesting animals.

TAMBORITO. A native dance and rhythm of Panama.

TAZAJO. Ox meat, which has been grilled, pounded thin, and served with a tomato sauce over it.

TEJEIRA, Alfonso. Born in 1903, Tejeira is an agronomist whose specialty is in chemical analysis of the soil. He received an A. E. degree from Cornell University, Ithaca, New York. He was a professor at the Universidad Nacional. He was also a delegate to the Inter-American Congress of Agriculture, Mexico City, 1942. In 1942 he also was on mission to the U. S. He served as 2nd secretary of the ministry of commerce and agriculture following his mission to the U. S.

TEJEMANEJE. An obfuscated, definitely illicit matter.

THOMSON-URRUTIA TREATY. This treaty, also called the Colombian Treaty, was ratified by the U. S. Senate on April 20, 1921. The United States was to pay Colombia $25 million for the loss of Panama and to grant free access to the Canal. Colombia recognized the independence of Panama and the boundaries, hitherto disputed, were adjusted. Diplomatic relations among Colombia, Panama, and the U. S. were regularized, and work began on various accords which were later to be signed in 1924-25. A similar treaty, in 1914, negotiated by the Wilson administration, had been defeated by the U. S. Congress, mainly on the strength of opposition by Theodore Roosevelt, who denounced it as blackmail.

TICOTACO. Hatred, ill-will, rivalry, a continuous alteration between two or more individuals.

TIERRA FIRME see CASTILLA DEL ORO.

TITBUA. A type of dove, also called tierrera or corralera.

TOLE. One of twelve distritos in the Province of Chiriquí. Its cabecera is Tolé.

TOLE. Cabecera of the Tolé District. Population: 597.

TONOSI. One of seven distritos in the Province of Los Santos. Its cabecera is Tonosí.

TONOSI. Cabecera of the Tonosí District. Population: 400.

TOTORRON see COCORRON.

TRAGANIQUEL. Any kind of slot machine, either for gambling or a vending machine or a "juke box."

TROJA. A type of granary built of very close-fitting, vertical cane stalks.

TRUCHO. Any animal with its tail or some other part of its body missing. Also, a person who has lost a small part of his body, e.g., one or more fingers or an ear.

TUCUTI RIVER. Sixth longest river in the country; 121 kilometers (76 miles) long, draining an area of 690 square kilometers. In the Province of Darién.

TUIRA RIVER. Fifth longest river in the country; 125 kilometers (79 miles) long, draining an area of 3,240 square kilometers. In the Province of Darién. Aside from the Chagres, which formed the lakes for the Canal, the Tuira River is probably the most important river commercially, as it serves as a transportation route for rafting hardwoods and fruits from the interior for shipment from the coastal ports.

TUMBAGA. An alloy, consisting of approximately 80% gold and 20% copper, used by pre-Hispanic Indians for casting various trinkets and objects. Found particularly in the Veraguas area, in the middle of western Panama between Chiriquí and Coclé. The indigenes used the cire perdue method of casting and also used the tumbaga for the manufacture of some relatively exquisite filigree work.

TUNA. In certain provinces, a street parade and carnival-like celebration by women wearing the pollera who, accompanied by musical instruments played by male companions, sing and dance native songs.

TURUMBA. A person who falls into stupefaction or confusion.

-U-

UNITED FRUIT COMPANY. This sprawling corporate giant was formed in 1899 by the merger of the Boston Fruit Company with several small tropical fruit companies owned and operated by M. O. Keith. Though the U. F. C. is often accused of meddling in the internal affairs of virtually all the Central American nations in which it has had operations, it has contributed appreciably in many ways to the fiscal betterment of most of the countries. The lowland areas of Central America, including Panama, were developed to produce bananas on a large scale while, simultaneously, the company developed its shipping and rail lines and distribution points. Although perhaps exploited at first, Panama has ultimately benefited by the operations of the Company, which first set up operations under its present name in 1899. Following near failure during the outbreak of Panama disease and sigatoka in the late 1920's and early 1930's, the banana industry has slowly come back to the point where, in 1960, the banana plantations of the United Fruit Company alone produced more than 7 million stems of bananas, valued at $11. 6 million.

UNITED NATIONS. Panama signed the United Nations Declaration on January 1, 1942. She offered assistance in the UN police action in Korea in 1952.

UNIVERSITY OF PANAMA. Founded May 29, 1935, the delightful campus and buildings housing the University's eight Faculties (colleges) and more than 8, 000 students, were completed in 1946. There are also extension and summer courses at the University Campus and in the Republic. The Colleges presently in operation are: Public Administration and Commerce; Architecture; Natural Sciences and Pharmacy; Law and Political Sciences; Humanities; Engineering;

Agronomy; and Medicine.

URABA. In 1508, a grant of land called Urabá was given
to Alonso de Ojeda. The land was located on the
Pearl Coast east of Panama. Ojeda founded the town
of San Sebastián, but in 1509 moved to a new site
and renamed it Santa María la Antigua del Darién.

URRIOLA, José Dolores, 1834-1883. "El mulato." A popular poet of Colombia and Panamá.

-V-

VAINA. A very frequently used expression in Panamanian
speech, used to insinuate something disagreeable,
not to one's liking, or even very enjoyable. Depend-
ent on the context in which used.

VAINAZO. Insult.

VALDES, Ramón M. A close follower of Dr. Belisario
Porras, Valdés came to power with Porras' backing
in 1916. He carried on all of Porras' programs and
is often considered to have been no more than a fig-
urehead president. He died in office in 1918 and
Porras once again was elected acting president.

VALDES ALVAREZ, Ignacio de Jesús. Valdés Alvarez was
born in Santiago, Panama in 1902. He was editor
of El Tiempo from 1924-1928 and editor-in-chief of
El Panamá América from 1928-1931. He was named
consul general, London, England (1931-34). He was
a radio commentator from 1934-1940 and supervisor
of press, radio, and public entertainment beginning
in 1940. He is the author of Vibraciones (1926),
Sangre Criolla (1943), and many others.

VELA VERDE. In the expression "decir hasta vela verde,"
means to acidly insult someone in the most cutting
of terms.

VENTA CRUZ. A town formerly located on the Chagres
River which served as a terminus for river boats
poled up the Chagres from Portobelo prior to the construction of the Canal. The town was also the northern end of the Panama-Venta Cruz Trail, another

transportation artery necessary for trans-Isthmian traffic prior to the Canal and railway.

VERAGUA see CASTILLA DEL ORO.

VERAGUAS. One of the nine provinces of Panama, located in the west-central part of the nation. Bordered by the Provinces of Chiriquí and Bocas del Toro on the west; by the Caribbean on the north; by the Provinces of Colón, Coclé, Herrera and Los Santos on the east; by the Pacific Ocean on the south and southwest. It has an area of 4,280 sq. mi. and its capital is the city of Santiago. The eleven distritos and their respective cabeceras are: Santiago, Santiago; Atalaya, Atalaya; Calobre, Calobre; Cañazas, Cañazas; La Mesa, La Mesa; Las Palmas, Las Palmas; Montijo, Montijo; Río de Jesús, Río de Jesús; San Francisco, San Francisco; Santa Fé, Santa Fe; Soná, Soná. Total population of the province (official estimate of 1969) is 161,100. The economy of this province is based on agriculture.

VERNON, Admiral Edward. A British admiral who, leading a huge expeditionary force, in 1739, captured Portobelo in the Darién and in 1740 sacked San Lorenzo. These actions were in connection with the "War of Jenkins' Ear" (1739), an encounter between Spain and England which had as its fuse the purported loss of an ear by a shipmaster by the name of Jenkins. This soon degenerated into the full-blown War of the Austrian Succession (1740-1748).

VERRUGOSA see MAPANA.

VICEROY. The crown's direct representative in the colonies and the highest colonial office. The viceroy was selected by the crown and the Council of Indies. He was usually a member of a high ranking family and usually held the office from three to five years. Viceroyalty duties were to enforce law, collect revenue, and convert the Indians. The viceroy appointed most officials, down to the minor posts. He granted the encomiendas in his territory. At the end of his term of office, his activities were reviewed by the Residencia, who had to approve his record. He was limited in his actions by the Audiencia, which functioned as an advisory council.

VICEROYALTY OF PERU. Created by the New Laws (1542)
   with its capital at Lima. Panama was a part of this
   Viceroyalty.

VILLALAZ, Carlos. Born in Panama City in 1900, Villalaz
   is well known as a portrait painter, poet and teacher.
   He attended Seton Hall University (South Orange, New
   Jersey), the University School (Southport, England),
   and the Academy of Arts (Liverpool). He received
   an A. B. from Cambridge University. He was Secretary to the governor of Colón in 1932, and acting
   mayor in 1932. He received a diploma of honor for
   a portrait of Mrs. Roosevelt at the Latin American
   Fair, New York, in 1942. He painted portraits of
   Panamanian presidents and designed the municipal
   insignia of Colón in 1927.

VIRREY see VICEROY.

VISITADOR. An official with unlimited power, appointed by
   the crown to visit the colonies and to investigate the
   viceroy or other officials during their terms of office.

VISITAFLOR. Hummingbird.

-Y-

YAYA. Used with verbs estar or poner en la, meaning to
   be in a bind. Also, to be under the influence of
   another.

YELLOW FEVER see GORGAS, Dr. Wm. C.

YUMECA. From English Jamaican. A popular name for
   Jamaican Negroes.

-Z-

ZAGAÑO. An insect similar to, but much larger than a
   honey bee.

ZANDUNGUERO. Lively, brisk, festive.

ZAPALLO see OYAMA.

ZARZO. In country homes, a rounded or quadrilateral
hanging shelf on which foodstuffs and utensils are
stored.

Bibliography

Alba C., Manuel María. Cronología de los gobernantes de Panamá: 1510-1967. Panamá, Ministerio de Educación, 1967.

Atlantic-Pacific Interoceanic Canal Study Commission. Fourth Annual Report, July 31, 1968. Washington, D. C., Government Printing Office, 1968.

Bannon, John Francis, S. J. and Peter Masten Dunne, S. J. Latin America: An Historical Survey. Milwaukee, The Bruce Publishing Company, 1958.

Bayitch, S. A. Latin America: A Bibliographical Guide. Coral Gables, Fla., University of Miami Press, 1961.

Biesanz, John, and Mavis Biesanz. The People of Panama. New York, Columbia University Press, 1955.

Cárdenas, Eduardo. 20, 000 biografías breves diccionario biográfico universal. Hanover, Pa., Libros de America, 1963.

Castillero Calvo, Alfredo. Estructuras sociales y económicos de Veragua desde sus orígenes históricos, Siglos XVI y XVII. Panamá, 1967.

Castillero R., Ernesto J. El Palacio de las Garzas: historia del palacio presidencial de Panamá. Tr. Luis C. Noli. Panamá, 1968.

_____. Historia de Panamá. 7a. ed. Panamá, Impresora Panamá, S. A., 1962.

Center for Strategic Studies, Georgetown University. Panama: Canal Issues and Treaty Talks. Washington, D. C., Center for Strategic Studies, 1967.

Chase, Gilbert. A Guide to the Music of Latin America. 2nd ed. Washington, D. C., Pan American Union, 1962.

Chong M., Moises. Historia de Panamá. Chitré, Ministerio de Educación, 1968.

Colon Free Zone: Decree Law No. 18, June 17, 1948: Decree No. 428 of September 7, 1953. Colón, 1968.

Contraloría General de la República. Panamá en cifras (compendio estadístico: años 1963 a 1967). Panamá, Comisión de Publicaciones, 1968.

Dame, Hartley F. Latin America 1969. Washington, D. C., Stryker-Post Publications, 1969.

Darío Carlos, Rubén. Crossing the Isthmus of Panamá. Tr. Phyllis Spencer. Panamá, MAC, 1946.

_____. Panamá. Tr. A. V. McGeachy. Panamá, Panamanian Tourist Board, 1962(?).

Dozer, Donald Marquand. Latin America. New York, McGraw-Hill Book Company, Inc., 1962.

DuVal, Miles P., Jr. And the Mountains Will Move: The Story of the Building of the Panama Canal. Stanford, Stanford University Press, 1947.

_____. Cadiz to Cathay: The Long Diplomatic Struggle for the Panama Canal. Stanford, Stanford University Press, 1947.

Encyclopedia Americana. Vol. 21. New York, Americana Corp., 1966.

Encyclopedia International. Vol. 14. New York, Grolier, Inc., 1964.

Fagg, John Edwin. Latin America. New York, The Macmillan Company, 1965.

Harrison John P. Guide to Materials on Latin America in the National Archives. Washington, D. C., Government Printing Office, 1961.

Hazelton, Alan Weaver. Eloy Alfaro: Apostle of Pan Americanism. Forest Hills, N. Y., Las Americas Publishing Co., 1943.

Instituto Panameño de Turismo. About the Canal. Mimeo.

102

Panamá, IPAT, 1968(?).

_____. Brief History of IPAT. Mimeo. Panamá, IPAT, 1969.

_____. El Montuno. Mimeo. Panamá, IPAT, 1968(?).

_____. La Pollera. Mimeo. Panamá, IPAT, 1968(?).

_____. Tourism. Panamá, IPAT, 1969.

Isaza Calderón, Baltásar and Ricardo J. Alfaro. Panameñismos. 2da. ed. Panamá, Impresora Panamá, S. A., 1968.

James, Herman G. and Percy A. Martin. The Republics of Latin America. New York, Harper and Brothers Publishers, 1923.

James, Preston E. Latin America. 3rd ed. New York, The Odyssey Press, 1959.

Keen, Benjamin, ed. Readings, in Latin American Civilization. Boston, Mass., Houghton Mifflin Company, 1967.

King, Joseph P., et al. The World and Its Peoples: The Caribbean Region and Central America. New York Greystone Press, 1965.

Langer, William L. An Encyclopedia of World History. Cambridge, Massachusetts, The Riverside Press, 1956.

Latin American Report. "Where Time Stood Still: San Blas Islands, Panama." A Latin American Report Special. New Orleans, ITM, n. d.

McCain, William D. The United States and The Republic of Panama. Durham, Duke University Press, 1937.

Mack, Gerstle. The Land Divided: A History of the Panama Canal and Other Isthmian Canal Projects. New York, Knopf, 1944.

Madden Dam: An integral part of the Panama Canal. Washington, D. C. (?), 1968.

Martin, Michael and G. H. Lovett. An Encyclopedia of Latin American History. New York, Abelard-Schuman, 1951.

Mexico and Central America. U. S. A., American Automobile Association, 1968.

Moore, Richard E. Historical Dictionary of Guatemala. Metuchen, N. J., The Scarecrow Press, Inc., 1967.

Munro, Dana Gardner. The Latin American Republics. New York, D. Appleton-Century Company, 1942.

Pan American Union. Panama. American Republics Series. No. 16. Washington, D. C., 1966.

Panama Canal Company. Fifteenth Annual Report, December 29, 1967. Washington, D. C., Government Printing Office, 1968.

Panama Canal Information Office. Basic Information on the Panama Canal. Panamá(?), 1968.

Reverte C., Manuel. El Matrimonio entre los indios Cuna de Panamá. 2da. ed. Panamá, 1967.

Rubio, Angel. Pequeño atlas geográfico de Panamá. 6a. ed. Panamá, Ediciones Oasis, S. A., 1963.

Statesman's Yearbook: Statistical & Historical Annual of the States of the World. 1968-1969. New York, St. Martin's Press, 1969.

Tribunal Electoral, República de Panama. Partidos nacionales y partidos municipales. Ms. Panama, 1969.

United States Department of Commerce. Basic Data on the Economy of Panama. Washington, D. C., Government Printing Office, 1968.

United States Department of State. Republic of Panama: Background Notes. Washington, D. C., U. S. Government Printing Office, 1968.

The West Indies and Caribbean Yearbook; Annuario comercial de las Antillas y países del Caribe. London, Thomas Skinner & Co. Ltd., 1969.

Whitted, Gerald W., ed. New Horizons World Guide (Pan Am Airways). New York, Simon and Schuster, Inc., 1969.

Who's Who in Latin America, A Biographical Dictionary of Notable Living Men and Women. Part 2, Central America and Panama. 3rd ed. Stanford University Press, 1945.

Wilgus, A. Curtis, ed. Eloy Alfaro 1842-1912: Citizen of the Americas. Panama City, Panama, Eloy Alfaro International Foundation, 1950.

Wilgus, A. Curtis. Historical Atlas of Latin America. New York, Cooper Square Publishers, Inc., 1967.

_____ and Raul d'Eca. Latin American History. New York, Barnes and Noble, Inc., 1969.

Worldmark Encyclopedia of the Nations. Americas. Edited by Louis Barron, New York, Worldmark Press, vol. 3, 1967.